LATE HAN CHINESE

LATE HAN CHINESE

A Study of the Archaic-Han Shift

W. A. C. H. DOBSON

Professor of Chinese and Head of the Department
of East Asian Studies, University of Toronto

UNIVERSITY OF TORONTO PRESS

© University of Toronto Press 1964

Printed in Canada

à

PAUL DEMIÉVILLE

Doyen des Sinologues

PREFACE

In writing this book, as with <u>Late Archaic Chinese</u> and <u>Early Archaic Chinese</u>, to which it is complementary, I have enjoyed the benefit of the advice of a number of scholars, too many to acknowledge in person. I gratefully record my thanks to them. I must, however, particularly thank Mr. A.H.C. Ward for valuable observations drawn from his own researches on the <u>Leu-shyh Chuen-chiou</u>, which he has allowed me to include. I am also indebted to Mrs. Betty Easterbrook who typed the manuscript and to Raymond Chu who wrote the Chinese characters.

This volume is a companion to <u>Late Archaic Chinese</u> and to <u>Early Archaic Chinese</u>. It has, however, been reproduced from typewritten manuscript by the photo-offset process, because of the peculiar difficulty of procuring the Chinese type necessary, and the consequent delay involved in using Chinese type.

I gratefully acknowledge the financial assistance provided by the Humanities Research Fund of the University of Toronto.

Finally in homage to Professor Paul Demiéville of the Collège de France, on his completing fifty years in the service of Sinology, this book is, with permission, respectfully dedicated to him.

W.A.C.H. Dobson

Massey College,
University of Toronto.
1964

CONTENTS

PREFACE   vii

INTRODUCTION   xiii

   (i) Aims and Objects   xiii
  (ii) History of the Study   xiii
 (iii) Late Han Literary Chinese   xvii
  (iv) Method and Statement   xx
   (v) Method and Procedure   xxi
 (vi) The Archaic Han Shift   xxiii

1. THE ARCHAIC-HAN SHIFT   3

2. SYNTAGMA   4

  2.1. The Personal Pronouns   4
    i. Obsolescence of Determinative Forms   4
  2.2. The Anaphoric Pronouns   5
    i. The Blunting of Distinctions   5
  2.3. The Demonstratives   6
    i. Obsolescence of Determinative Forms   6
    ii. <u>Chyi</u> as a Demonstrative   7
    iii. <u>Chyi</u> in <u>Chyi-shyr</u> etc.   8
    iv. <u>Chyi</u> before <u>Ren</u>   8
  2.4. Collectives and Restrictives   9
    i. Shift in meaning of <u>Farn</u>   9
    ii. <u>Dann</u> before Nouns   10
  2.5. The Particle of Syntagma   11
    i. <u>Jee</u> as a marker of Cause   11
  2.6. The Particle of Determination   11
    i. Blunting of usage   11
  2.7. Syntagma in Summary   12

3. THE VERB   14

  3.1. Mood   14
    i. The reduction of the role of the
      Modal Negatives to negation   14
    ii. The blunting of the Modal Negatives   16
    iii. Stressed or Intensive Negatives are
      replaced by periphrastic forms   16
    iv. Modification in meaning of <u>Wey</u>   17
    v. The blunting of the Modal role of
      <u>Guoo</u> and <u>Guh</u>   18
    vi. The replacement of <u>Yeou</u> and <u>Wei</u> in
      the Subjunctive   19

CONTENTS

  vii. The marking of the Injunctive   20
  viii. The use of <u>Shiu</u> and <u>Ing</u>   21
  ix. The modal functions of <u>Kee</u> and <u>Neng</u>   23
 3.2. Aspect   23
  i. Shifts in Potential and Momentary Aspect   23
  ii. Perfective Aspect   24
  iii. The use of <u>Fuh</u> for Durative and Iterative Aspect   25
  iv. <u>Dann</u> and Aspect   26
  v. <u>Dann</u> and Polarity   27
  vi. The use of <u>Jyi</u> and <u>Biann</u>   29
  vii. The use of <u>Meei</u> and <u>Jer</u>   30
 3.3. Manner   31
  i. The misinterpretation of <u>Yan</u>   31
  ii. The interpretation of '<u>yeou-attribute</u>' and '<u>attribute/sy</u>'   32
 3.4. Voice   32
  i. The <u>Jiann</u> Passive   33
  ii. The <u>Bey</u> Passive   34
  iii. The Periphrastic Passive in <u>Wei</u>   35
  iv. Causative and permissive   36
  v. <u>Tzay</u> as a post-verbal particle   37
 3.5. Direction   38
  i. <u>Tzyh</u> is replaced by <u>Tsorng</u>   38
  ii. <u>You</u> is replaced by <u>Tsorng</u>   39
 3.6. Polarity   39
  i. The obsolescence of the polar form '<u>negative/substitute/verb</u>'   39
  ii. <u>Dann</u> and Polarity   40
 3.7. The Verb in Summary   41

4. AGENCY   44

 4.1. The Pronouns   44
  i. Obsolescence of the agentive forms of the Pronouns   44
 4.2. The Distributives   45
  i. The obsolescence of <u>Huoh</u> and <u>Moh</u>   45
  ii. The encroachment of <u>Jiu</u> upon <u>Jie</u> and <u>Jie</u>   47
  iii. <u>Jiu</u> as a Collective   48
  iv. <u>Shwu</u> is assimilated into <u>Shwei</u>   48
  v. The use of <u>Shyan</u>   48
 4.3. Reciprocity   49
  i. The obsolescence of <u>Jiau</u> and the parasitic use of <u>Shiang</u>   49
 4.4. Delegated Agency   50
  i. <u>Wey</u> encroaches upon <u>Wey</u>   50
 4.5. The Reflexive   51
  i. The use of <u>Tzyh</u> in compounds   51

CONTENTS xi

  ii. The use of the Emphatic and Reflexive
    Pronoun <u>Jii</u>   52
 4.6. Agency in Summary   54

5. CLAUSES, PHRASES AND ENDINGS IN THE
  VERBAL SENTENCE   56

 5.1. The <u>Erl</u> Clause   56
  i. Diminution in the role of <u>Erl</u>   56
  ii. The use of the <u>Jih</u> Clause   58
 5.2. The Instrumental   58
  i. <u>Erl</u> terminating the Instrumental Clause   58
 5.3. Anaphora   59
  i. The use of Anaphora   59
  ii. The eroding of the Anaphoric Pronouns
    in allegro forms   61
 5.4. The Final Particles   64
  i. The loss of precision   64
  ii. The use of <u>Foou</u> and <u>Ran</u>   65
  iii. <u>Foou</u> and <u>Bu</u> as final interrogatives   66
 5.5. Time and Place   67
  i. <u>Shyi</u> becomes obsolescent   67
  ii. Miscellaneous   67
 5.6. The Verbal Sentence in Summary   69

6. THE DETERMINATIVE SENTENCE   71

 6.1. The Copulae   71
  i. <u>Shyh</u> as a Copula   71
  ii. <u>Dann</u> as a Copula   72
  iii. <u>Jyi</u> as a Copula   72
  iv. The Compounding of the Copulae of
    Common Inclusion   73
 6.2. Cause and Consequence   73
  i. The use of <u>Yuan</u>   73
 6.3. The Determinative Sentence in Summary   74

7. CONJUNCTIONS   75

 7.1. Co-ordinate sequence   75
  i. <u>Fuh</u> as a Co-ordinate Conjunction   75
  ii. The Adversative   76
  iii. The use of <u>Faan</u> "on the contrary"   77
 7.2. Conditioned Sequence   79
  (a) Marking the protasis   79
  i. <u>Ru-shyy</u>, <u>ru</u>, <u>jea-shyy</u>, and <u>shyy</u>   79
  ii. <u>Cherng</u> replaces <u>Goou</u>   80
  (b) Marking the apodosis   81
  iii. <u>Tzer</u> replaces <u>Sy</u>   81
  iv. <u>Tzer</u> replaced by <u>Tsyy</u> or <u>Dang</u>   81
  v. <u>Jiow</u> in Conditioned Sequences   81

CONTENTS

7.3. Concession	82
i. The use of *Tzyh*	82
ii. *Taang* as a concessive conjunction	83
iii. The use of *Shanq* in Concession	83
7.4. Conjunctions in Summary	85
8. SUBSTITUTION	**87**
8.1. The Pronouns	87
i. The Personal Pronouns	87
ii. The Anaphoric Pronouns	88
8.2. The Demonstratives	89
8.3. The Interrogative Substitutes	89
i. The assimilation by *An* of *Yan* and *U* and *U-hu*	90
ii. The use of *Ninq*	91
iii. The assimilation of *Shwu* by *Shwei*	92
iv. The obsolescence of *Shi*	92
v. Expansions of LAC *Her*	92
vi. Changes in the syntactical deployment of the Interrogative Substitutes	94
vii. The use of *Chii*	94
viii. The use of *Tserng*	95
8.4. Substitution in Summary	95
9. MISCELLANEOUS	**97**
1. The Degrees of Comparison	97
2. The Allegro Forms	99
3. Enumeration	99
4. Miscellaneous in Summary	100
10. CONCLUSION	**101**
POSTSCRIPT	**103**
APPENDIXES	
I. Late Han and Early Archaic Chinese	105
II. The Nature of Late Han Classical Chinese	109
III. Late Han and Modern Standard Chinese	112
IV. Jaw Chyi's notions about Language	115
LIST OF WORKS MENTIONED	**119**
INDEX OF WORDS TREATED AT SOME LENGTH	**121**

INTRODUCTION

(i) Aims and Objects

The present work is a comparative study of the grammar of two stages in the evolution of "Classical Chinese." More particularly, it is a detailed study of a 3rd Century B.C. text (Late Archaic Chinese) and of a paraphrase of that text in the language of the 2nd Century A.D. (Late Han Literary Chinese). The comparison is made in an attempt to explore the nature of evolutionary change in the language, by comparing samples of two periods which have a common subject-matter. If these two samples prove to be typical, and there is good reason to think that they are,[1] then a fundamental shift occurs in the language between Late Archaic and Late Han. It is the purpose of the present work to describe that shift - - the Archaic-Han-Shift - - as a contribution towards an historical treatment of the grammar of Archaic and Classical Chinese.

(ii) History of the Study

The present study is a continuation of, and a further stage in, a long-term programme of research. This programme began with an attempt to devise a purely formal system for describing the grammar of Archaic Chinese. The system was then applied, period by period, in a series of diachronic descriptive grammars of Archaic Chinese. Three periods were set up: Early, Middle and Late Archaic Chinese. By comparing the variables period by period, the rough shape of evolutionary change within Archaic Chinese was then sketched. The present study

---

[1] See paragraph iii below.

adds a further period - - Late Han, and a further set of variables - - the differences observable by these methods between Late Archaic and Late Han Literary Chinese. At a further stage, it is proposed to add more periods and to make further comparisons. At an ultimate stage, the periodization can be refined, the changes more closely observed,[2] even accurately dated, and the study will then culminate in a synchronic Grammar of Classical Chinese - - from its "classical" beginnings to the wide variety of forms which, though patterned on classical models, in fact emerged, and comprise what is generically called "Classical Chinese."

The present study is thus only meaningful when taken with its predecessors. In *Late Archaic Chinese*[3] the possibility of describing the grammar of Archaic Chinese by strictly formal and observable criteria was explored. Analytical procedure was based on the observation that the Archaic Chinese "word" (which is incapable of inflexion or of change of "phonological shape"),[4] varies in its reference and function as it assumes various relationships with other "words." Classes were set up in terms of sets of relationships - -

---

[2] See postscript.

---

[3] W.A.C.H. Dobson, *Late Archaic Chinese* (Toronto 1959), abbreviated hereafter as *LAC*.

---

[4] With the exception of phonological change at the lexical level as a process of word derivation, see *LAC* Appendix 1.

INTRODUCTION   xv

"frames" or "matrices" - - in which the otherwise un-
changing word can be observed to occur.[5]

In LAC this system was applied in presenting a diachronic description of the grammar of a sampling of
Archaic Chinese authors of the 4th and 3rd Centuries
B.C. This language was characterized as Late Archaic
Chinese (= LAC). In Early Archaic Chinese[6] the degree
of predictability of the system was tested by applying
it to a corpus of bronze inscriptions of the 11th and
10th Centuries B.C. The language of these inscriptions
has hitherto been little understood. This language,
characterized as Early Archaic Chinese (= EAC), is also
the language of the Wuu Gaw (五誥), traditionally
thought to be the "most genuine" of the books of the
Shu Jing.

In an Appendix to EAC[7] features of EAC and LAC were
placed side by side in order to explore the nature of
evolutionary change in the language from the 11th-10th
Centuries to the 4th-3rd Centuries B.C. Further, by

---

[5] See "Word Classes or Distributional Classes in
Archaic Chinese"; in "L'Hommage à Monsieur Demiéville"
(in press).

---

[6] W.A.C.H. Dobson, Early Archaic Chinese (Toronto
1962), abbreviated hereafter as EAC.

---

[7] EAC Appendix 1, "Towards a Historical Treatment
of the Grammar of Archaic Chinese."

making a diachronic descriptive study of the Spring and Autumn Annals[8] - - a text poised in time somewhere between EAC and LAC and set up provisionally as Middle Archaic Chinese (=MAC) - - it was possible to explore the nature of evolutionary change further. With the features of three samplings of three periods within Archaic Chinese compared, discernible shifts and changes were apparent as the language progresses from Early to Middle and from Middle to Late Archaic Chinese. These shifts and changes were examined in depth and detail in a study of one grammatical feature in an article "Early Archaic yüeh > Late Archaic chi."[9] In the present study the process of taking samples of periodical "cuts" in the language and submitting them to analysis and comparison has been continued.

The present study therefore assumes the postulates of previous studies.[10] The system of analysis, its terminology, the "sampling method," the organization of the

---

[8] W.A.C.H. Dobson, "Studies in Middle Archaic Chinese - - The Spring and Autumn Annals," T'oung Pao (1963) L. 1-3, pp. 221-238.

---

[9] W.A.C.H. Dobson "Towards a Historical Treatment of the Grammar of Archaic Chinese - - Early Archaic Yüeh > Late Archaic Chi," HJAS 23 (1961) pp. 5-18.

---

[10] To the above-mentioned studies should be added: W.A.C.H. Dobson, "Studies in the Grammar of Early Archaic Chinese, I, The Particle Wei," T'oung Pao XLVI (1958) pp. 339-368; and "Studies in the Grammar of Early Archaic Chinese, II, The Word Jo," T'oung Pao XLVII (1959) pp. 281-293.

descriptive statement, etc., are all part of an integral and consistent whole. This study is only understandable in the terms in which its predecessors were made.

(iii) Late Han Literary Chinese

"Late Han Literary Chinese" (= Late Han) like its predecessors, "Early Archaic Chinese," "Middle Archaic Chinese" and "Late Archaic Chinese," is an analyst's abstraction. It is, in fact, the "idiolect" of one writer of the Late Han period and in particular the language he uses when translating Archaic Chinese into a simple literary form of Chinese current in his day. He also uses, for didactic purposes and in a quite separate context, a highly contrived "classical" style, which I have called "Late Han Classical Chinese." The latter draws deliberately on archaic forms and usages while the former, as deliberately, avoids archaic usage. When therefore mention is made in this study of "Late Han," it must be understood in this accommodated sense. It is in fact Late Han usage as represented by one author in one text that has been scientifically analysed. Similarly, a number of grammatical features have been described as "Late Han innovations." This again must be understood in an accommodated sense. They are innovations as far as Archaic Chinese is concerned, but they may well have antedated our Late Han author.[11]

The "sample" is a paraphrase with extended commentary on a text of some 35,226 words. It must contain something like a 100,000 words. The extent to which it is typical of other Late Han authors is yet to be determined, but most of its innovations (as notes scattered

---

[11] See postscript.

xviii INTRODUCTION

throughout this book indicate[12]) are common to such Late Han writers as Jenq Shyuan (鄭玄) (127-200 A.D.), Wei Jau (韋昭) (204-273 A.D.), Gaw Yeow (高誘) (2nd Cent. A.D.) and Wang Yih (王逸) (fl. 2nd Cent. A.D.) when writing in similar vein.[13] But, when writing in Late Han Classical Chinese, our author uses a style, vocabulary and grammatical forms very similar to those of the Han writer Ban Guh (班固) (39-92 A.D.). Details in the description of "Late Han Literary Chinese" and of "Late

---

[12] See 2.2.i footnote; 3.1.v Note; 3.2.i Note; 3.5.i Note; 4.3.i Note; 5.4.iii Note; 5.5.i Note; and 5.5.ii.

---

[13] Examples cited from the works of these Late Han writers have been culled from the critical apparatus of Jiau Shyun (焦循) in his Menq-tzyy jenq-yih (孟子正義.) A.H.C. Ward has made a detailed study of the Commentary (注) of Gaw Yeou (高誘) on the Leu-shyh Chuen-chiou (呂氏春秋). He has kindly supplied the following examples from Gaw Yeou, in addition to those cited in Jiau Shyun's Commentary. 人 > 他人 (cf. 2.3.iv); 勿 > 無 (cf. 3.1.i); 特 > 但 (cf. 3.2.iv); 乎 > 於 (cf. 3.4.v); 自 > 從 (cf. 3.5.i); 奚自 > 何從 (cf. 3.5.i); 由 > 從 (cf. 3.5.ii) 無或 > 無有 (cf. 4.2.i); 咸 > 皆 (cf. 4.2.ii); 孰 > 誰 (cf. 4.2.iv); 繄 > 即 (cf. 5.4.i); 還間 and 少選 > 須臾 (cf. 5.5.ii); 還間 is glossed as 猶還頃也 and 間 in 居有間 as 頃 (cf. 5.5.ii); 安 > 異 (cf. 5.5.ii); 猶 > 尚 (cf. 7.3.iii); 若 > 汝 and 而 > 汝 (cf. 8.1.i); 惡 > 安, 惡用 > 安用 and 奚 > 何 (cf. 8.3.iv); both 愈 and 彌 > 益 (cf. 9.1.); 茲 > 此 (cf. App. II). He also notes: as agential distributive 畢 > 盡; as noun 始 > 初; as verb 以 > 用 and 殆 > 必; 幾 "nearly" > 近 and 微 "if it were not for" > 無.

INTRODUCTION   xix

Han Classical Chinese" may need modification in the light
of further researches, but as an interim stage, the
assumption that the sample is typical is a useful one,
since it enables us to plot the main outlines of evolutionary change from Archaic to Han.

   The sample of Late Han Literary Chinese is taken
from the Menq-tzyy Jang jiuh 孟子章句 of Jaw Chyi 趙岐
(d. 201 A.D.). The Jang-jiuh consists of Chapter
Summaries - - the Jang-jyy 章指 - - and of a Commentary
- - the Juh 注 - - upon the text of Mencius. Jaw Chyi
has arranged the text into "chapters" jang 章 and divided
the chapters into sentences and paragraphs jiuh 句.
Hence his title - - Jang-jiuh. The Chapter Summaries
appear at the end of each chapter, and the Commentary is
interspersed between paragraphs and sentences.

   The language used by Jaw Chyi for the Commentary is
quite different from the language used for the Chapter
Summaries. The Commentary consists largely of paraphrase. Jaw Chyi says in his Preface[14] that the Commentary was prepared for those "beginning their studies."
The language of Mencius was already five hundred years
old in Jaw Chyi's time. Its archaisms would occasion a
beginner difficulty. His purpose in using paraphrase
was expository and the language he uses for exposition
is clearly the sort of "easy wen-yan" that those
"beginning their studies" in the Late Han period would
understand. The paraphrase is, in short, translation
from Late Archaic Chinese into Late Han Literary Chinese.
The Chapter Summaries, on the other hand, are homiletical
in character. They are written in a highly contrived and

----

   [14] See Menq-tzyy Tyi-tsyr (孟子題辭) (page 24)
in Menq-tzyy Jenq-yih, for details of which see para.
iv below.

lapidary style. They use the four-stress line, and are replete with archaic usages drawn indifferently from the Classics of all periods of Archaic Chinese.[15] The Commentary, by contrast, studiously avoids archaic usages as being incompatible with its avowed purpose and keeps to contemporary forms.

For the purposes previously mentioned the language of the Commentary is characterized as "Late Han Literary Chinese," and the language of the Chapter Summaries as "Late Han Classical Chinese," since the language of the latter is deliberately imitative of the language of the Classics, while the former, as deliberately, avoids classical usage because it is its aim to explain such usage.[16]

(iv) Method and Statement

As already mentioned above, this study is a further stage in a long-term programme of research. It makes certain procedural assumptions, is conducted by certain analytical procedures, and follows a consistent pattern in descriptive statement. For a description and discussion of them the reader is referred to the Introductions to Late Archaic Chinese and to Early Archaic Chinese.

---

[15] A listing is given in Appendix II.

---

[16] Yoshikawa Kōjirō says "It is logical to suppose that the modes of expression which later appeared in the New Anecdotes were already flourishing in the colloquial of Later Han times, but if so, Pan Ku admitted none of them whatsoever" ("SHIH-SHUO HSIN-YÜ and Six Dynasties Prose Style" translated by Glen Baxter HJAS 18 (1955), pp. 124-141). Most of the features

INTRODUCTION   xxi

    Systems of romanization and conventional signs and abbreviations follow the pattern standardized in the above-mentioned works. References in this work to the "Text" refer to the text of Mencius as published in the Menq-tzyy Jenq-yih, 孟子正義 of Jiau Shyun 焦循 (1763-1820). References to the "Commentary" 注 are to the Commentary of Jaw Chyi, as it appears in the Jenq-yih. Pagination for examples is given by section (tseh 册) and page number of the edition of the Jenq-yih published in the 國學基本叢書簡篇 (Basic Sinological Series (Shorter Collection)). A page reference followed by the character 章 refers to the Chapter Summaries 章指 appearing at the end of each chapter in the Jenq-yih.

(v) Method and Procedure

    In the present study the language of the Commentary has been analysed according to the procedures described in Late Archaic Chinese. The resulting description was then compared with the description of Mencius as given in LAC. In that comparison certain forms in the Text were seen consistently to be replaced in the Commentary, while others were, as consistently, retained, and

---

Yoshikawa describes (俱 "both"; 欲 "potential"; 寧可 "interrogative"; 耶 "final"; 相 and 復 in parasitic usage; and 是 "copula") are present in Jaw Chyi and thus were, as he supposes, current in Han times. Features described by Yoshikawa not attested by Jaw Chyi are 輒 "for his part" (Jaw Chyi uses 輒 "each time"); 便 "and" (Jaw Chyi uses 便 "at once"); and the intensive negatives 定不 and 都不 which do not occur in the Commentary at all. Whether such features were "colloquial" or not is a matter on which most linguists would hesitate to hazard an opinion. I have supposed them to be prima facie features of a simple literary style.

further, it was observed that the <u>Commentary</u> had forms and usages unknown in the language of the <u>Text</u>. These features were then abstracted. They constitute a catalogue of (i) features of Late Archaic Chinese still current in Late Han; (ii) features of Late Archaic Chinese obsolescent in Late Han; and (iii) innovations of usage in Late Han. Such a catalogue provides a measure of the nature and extent of evolutionary change in the five hundred years that elapse between the language of the <u>Text</u> and that of its paraphrase.

Description in this book takes the form of a report on the differences, level by level, and element by element, between LAC and Late Han. Description is developed in the hierarchical order followed in <u>LAC</u>. Taken together, these individual differences form a consistent pattern. This pattern, which has been characterized as the "Archaic-Han Shift," is summarized in Chapter 10. <u>Mencius</u> quotes extensively from the <u>Shu Jing</u> (書經) and the <u>Shy Jing</u> (詩經). Jaw Chyi paraphrases these citations. In Appendix I the differences between EAC and Late Han as it is revealed in these paraphrases are described. The differences reflect precisely the same tendencies as a comparison of LAC and Late Han reveal. Mention has already been made of the difference in language between Late Han Literary Chinese and Late Han Classical Chinese as shewn by Jaw Chyi's use of the latter for homiletical purposes. An analysis of this "Late Han Classical Chinese" is given in Appendix II. Finally, many of the features of the "Archaic-Han Shift" foreshadow the emergence of features of Modern Standard Chinese. The most suggestive of these are summarized in Appendix III. Finally, Jaw Chyi in his <u>Commentary</u> has a number of observations of a philological nature. From these something can be deduced about Chinese ideas on language in the 2nd Century A.D. These are described in Appendix IV.

(vi) The Archaic-Han Shift

A comparison of the contrastive features of Early, Middle and Late Archaic Chinese has shewn that almost the entire repertory of grammatical auxiliaries undergoes change between the 11th and the 3rd Centuries B.C. But while this is so, EAC, MAC and LAC retain common characteristics. The main burden of grammatical indication lies with the "empty words." The "full words" keep largely to single forms and enjoy a wide measure of syntactical ambivalence.

A comparison of the contrastive features of LAC and Late Han, on the other hand, shews a radical and fundamental shift. It is not merely, as with Archaic Chinese, that individual forms evolve and change, but that a fundamental shift takes place in the respective roles of the "empty" and "full words." The Archaic-Han Shift is away from the precise, predictable and major role of the "empty words" of Archaic Chinese in making grammatical distinctions towards the use of periphrastic means for making these distinctions in Late Han. The consequent loss in both role and meaning of the "empty words" is accompanied by greater complexity in the "full words." The trend is towards compound rather than single forms and to greater restriction in syntactical deployment, so that the degree of ambivalence between nounal, adjectival, verbal and adverbal usage of the "full words" of Archaic Chinese is greatly reduced by Late Han. The "full words" in their compounded forms tend to be deployed either as nouns or as verbs - and not to permutate.

Evolutionary change, as it occurs throughout Archaic Chinese, is a change in _form_ but not in _role_ for the "empty words." But, as the language passes through the Archaic-Han Shift, the <u>role</u> of the "empty words" as a class is changed. The role of grammatical indication passes to some extent to the "full words" in their new and more complex forms.

Quite clearly in the critical five hundred years from LAC to Late Han a change of the greatest importance in the historical evolution of the language takes place. We might say that the characterization of the grammatical auxiliaries of Chinese as "empty words" in Archaic Chinese is a misnomer, but, once the Archaic-Han Shift takes place, the characterization becomes appropriate. Many of the changes of the Archaic-Han Shift are towards features familiar in Modern Standard Chinese. The "Archaic-Han Shift" therefore marks a critical stage in the path of evolutionary progress in the language. At this critical stage the language reaches, as it were, a fork in the road. One literary form of the language (Late Han Literary Chinese) is contemporary, keeps abreast of change, and moves perceptibly towards Modern Chinese. Another form (Late Han Classical Chinese) is conservative, deliberately retaining, under the influence of canonical authority, archaic forms and features. But both forms, literary and classical, in some degree reflect contemporary change. Late Han Classical Chinese is not a pure imitation of Archaic Chinese. It is a form in which archaic features give an antique effect. Late Han Literary Chinese avoids these archaisms. But both forms, Literary and Classical, betray themselves by certain innovations typical of the period as Late Han languages.

LATE HAN CHINESE

CHAPTER 1

THE ARCHAIC HAN SHIFT

Jaw Chyi's paraphrase of Mencius provides the historian of the grammar of the Chinese language with a most valuable source of information. Placed side by side with the text of <u>Mencius</u>, it is an almost perfect index of evolutionary change in the language from the 3rd Century B.C. to the 2nd Century A.D.

In the chapters which follow these changes are described, level by level, and element by element. In Chapter 2 changes at the syntagmatic level, in Chapters 3-6 changes at the sentential level and in Chapter 7 changes at the intersentential level are described. In Chapters 8 and 9 changes that occur in substitution and certain other features, best treated by an inter-level approach, are also described. At the end of each chapter a summary of change is given. In their totality these changes can be described more generally and this is done in Chapter 10.

CHAPTER 2

S Y N T A G M A

In syntagma, or word-group formation, the principal changes in Late Han from LAC usage are: (i) the blurring of the distinction made in LAC between the determinative forms and the pregnant forms of the pronouns and demonstratives (see 2.1-2.3); (ii) shifts between pronominal and demonstrative usage (see 2.3.ii-iv); (iii) semantic change in a collective and the introduction of a new restrictive (see 2.4); (iv) another role for the particle of syntagma jee 者 (see 2.5); and (iv) blunting in the use of the particle of determination jy 之 (see 2.6).

2.1. The Personal Pronouns

i. Obsolescence of Determinative Forms

In LAC a distinction is made in the personal pronouns between determinative and pregnant usage. In the first person the determinative form is wu 吾 and the pregnant form is woo 我. In the second person the determinative form is eel 爾 and the pregnant form is ruu 汝 (see LAC 2.6.4.1). Wu, woo, and eel occur in Late Han in the determinative role, with that role marked by the particle of determination jy 之. This collocation of pronoun plus determinative particle (吾之；我之；爾之 etc.) is unknown to LAC. Wu and eel have clearly lost their distinctively determinative role (see also section 4.1.i below, where the determinative pronouns lose their agentive role also).

Examples

敬吾之老亦敬人之老愛我之幼亦愛人之幼 "We should respect our own aged and too

respect the aged of others. We should love our own young ones and too love the young ones of others." (1.58)

Text 吾浩然之氣 "my greater physical vigour" becomes 我之所有浩然之大氣也 "the greater physical vigour which I have" (2.61); compare also 我之教命 "my instructions" (2.9); 我之愆 "my fault" (3.37) 我之功 "my merit" (5.83) 於我之身 "in my person" (5.73); 夫射遠而至爾努力也其中的者爾之巧也 "to attain distance when shooting with a bow is a matter of your physical strength, but to score a bull's eye is a matter of your skill." (6.7)

Note. Jaw Chyi often paraphrases direct speech as indirectly reported speech. The pronouns of direct address therefore occur less frequently in the Commentary than in the Text. This makes it difficult to collect an adequate sample of the use of the personal pronouns. For example, in 6.74 the Text reads 曰吾弟則愛之秦人之弟則不愛也,是以我為悅者也故謂之內 "[Kao Tzu] said 'I feel love for my younger brother, but I feel no love for the younger brother of a man of Ch'in. And so, because [my brother] provokes a feeling of pleasure within me, I therefore say it [love] is internal.'" This in paraphrase becomes 告子曰愛從己則己心悅,故謂之內 "Kao Tzu said that love proceeded from himself and so his own heart felt pleasure. Therefore he called [love] internal." Of some 30 determinative usages of wu in the Text, for example, only two are paraphrased in direct speech.

2.2. The Anaphoric Pronouns

i. The Blunting of Distinctions

In LAC, the anaphoric pronouns (chyi 其 in the determinative form and <u>jy</u> 之 in the pregnant form) are strictly differentiated (see <u>LAC</u> 3.8). In Late Han, this differentiation is occasionally blurred.[1] <u>Jy</u> occurs where, in LAC, <u>chyi</u> would occur.

Examples
Text: 勿視其巍巍然
Commentary: 勿敢視之巍巍 "disregard their awesomeness" (8.100); in the <u>Commentary</u> 當本之志 is in parallel with 不可...害其辭 "you should take for your basis [of interpretation] <u>its</u> [i.e. the poem's] intention ... you cannot ... do violence to <u>its</u> phrasing" (5.101); 故民從之教化輕易也 "Therefore the people follow his teaching with ease" (1.68); <u>Ju</u> 諸 is used in Late Han for <u>jy</u> 之 (see 5.3.ii below). In the following <u>chyi</u> not <u>jy</u> would be LAC usage.[2] 比諸見放也 "by the time that he was exiled" (5.93); 禦人以兵禦人而奪之貨 "a highwayman is one who detains people by force of arms and takes away <u>their</u> property" (6.28).

2.3. The Demonstratives
 i. Obsolescence of Determinative Forms
 Although, in LAC, the demonstrative <u>tsyy</u> 此 is used determinatively (for example 此極 "these extremities" as

---

[1] The blunted use of <u>chyi</u> in other Han authors has been noted by Leu Shwu-shiang 呂叔湘. See <u>Hann-yeu yeu-fa Luen-wen Jyi</u> 漢語語法論文集 (Peking 1955), p. 181.

[2] For examples of "<u>bih chyi</u> verb" (比其/3) see W.A.C.H. Dobson "Towards a Historical Treatment of the Grammar of Archaic Chinese - - Early Archaic <u>Yüeh</u> > Late Archaic <u>Chi</u>," HJAS 23 (1961), pp. 5-6.

in 1.77), the form restricted to determination is sy 斯 (see LAC 2.6.4.2). In Late Han, sy is replaced by tsyy. This suggests that forms of the demonstrative restricted to the determinative role are obsolescent in Late Han. (Sy as a conditional conjunction in LAC is also obsolescent in Late Han and is replaced by tzer 則; see 7.2.iv below.)

Examples
斯 is replaced by 此 in 4.86; 1.34; 1.109; 5.119 (將 for 斯 in some editions is a misprint).

The two demonstratives of Late Han tsyy 此 and shyh 是 both occur in determinative usage, sporadically, with the particle of determination jy 之.

Examples
Tsyy jy occurs in 如此之用 "usages of this kind" (7.50). Shyh jy occurs in 於是之際 "in these extremities" (7.101 (章)).

ii. Chyi as a Demonstrative

An innovation in Late Han is the extended use of the determinative anaphoric pronoun chyi as a demonstrative before certain nouns. In this usage, chyi bears a resemblance to the Modern Standard Chinese jehgeh and jehyanqde (這個 and 這樣的), for example, chyi might be translated jehyanqde in 眾皆悅美之，其人自以所行為是而無仁義之實 "The crowd all like and admire him. This sort of person thinks his own course of conduct is right, but he lacks the reality of Humanity and Justice." (8.117) And in the following example chyi might be translated jehgeh. 我不絜其人之行,故不教誨之,其人感此,退自修學而為仁義,是亦我教誨之一道也 "I do not think this person's conduct is pure and so I do not teach him. But such a man will be affected by this, and, retiring from my presence, cultivate learning on his own and so become Humane and Just. This, too, is one way for me to teach him." (7.66)

Examples
Other examples of <u>chyi</u> as a demonstrative are 而其人 "yet such a man" (<u>7.85</u>); 其國君臣 "the princes and ministers of these states" (<u>8.67</u>); 喜其人 "pleased that this man's ..." (7.54); 得其人舉之 "obtained such a man and promoted him" (<u>7.59</u>); 其井田之大要 "The essential points of this well-field system" (<u>3.82</u>). See also 1.53.

iii. <u>Chyi</u> in <u>Chyi-shyr</u> etc.
<u>Chyi</u> also occurs before <u>shyr</u> 實 in <u>chyi-shyr</u> 其實 "The fact of the matter is ...," "In reality ...," and in <u>chyi-jong</u> 其終, "In the end ...," "finally ..."

Examples
其實但為合眾之行 "In reality, this is merely conforming with the crowd" (<u>8.115</u>); 是以其終亦皆弒其君 "So that, in the end, all of them assassinated their princes" (1.10). See also 5.62 (章).

iv. <u>Chyi</u> before <u>Ren</u>
In LAC <u>ren</u> 人 "man" often occurs in a pronominal usage in the sense of "other than the person speaking or the person addressed, others, etc," as for example, 則人將曰 "then others will say" (7.55). In the translation of this passage into Late Han, it is rendered 則其人將曰 "then others [= <u>chyi-ren</u>] will say" and the passage continues 訑訑賤他人之言 "How smug he is! He regards what others say with contempt" (7.56). Here both <u>chyi-ren</u> and <u>ta-ren</u> occur for "other men." Before this pronominal <u>ren</u> both <u>chyi</u> and <u>ta</u> are synonymous. <u>Chyi</u> in the sense of "other, the rest" also occurs in <u>chyi-yu</u> 其餘 .

SYNTAGMA

Examples

Late Han uses <u>ta-ren</u> for pronominal <u>ren</u> in 8.7; 6.126; etc. Other nouns determined by <u>ta</u> are 他國 "another State" (7.30); 他辭 "some other excuse" (6.27); 他事 "other things" (2.3); 他故 "some other reason" (5.10). <u>Chyi-yu</u> occurs in 此二者猶天下之父也其餘皆天下之子耳 "These two elderly statesmen were, as it were, the fathers of the Empire, the rest being all the Empire's children" (4.103); and determinatively in 其餘指 "the other fingers" (6.116).

Thus, <u>chyi</u>, a pronoun in LAC, becomes, in Late Han (a) confused with its pregnant form <u>jy</u>, (b) extended in usage as a demonstrative "this, this sort of" and (c) from a contrastive form with <u>ta</u> (<u>chyi</u> "this," <u>ta</u> "the other") becomes assimilated with <u>ta</u> as "other." <u>Chyi</u> in this latter usage has an echo in the modern <u>chyitade</u> 其他的 "the other, others."

<u>Note</u>. It is difficult not to suspect an historical connection between the LAC demonstrative <u>sy</u> 斯, its repression in Late Han times, and the occurrence in Late Han of a <u>chyi</u> 其 demonstrative. Again the occasional 其-之 confusion in Late Han, and the occurrence of <u>chyi</u> as a demonstrative, recall the use of <u>jy</u> 之 as a determinative demonstrative in LAC, which is peculiar to <u>Juang-tzyy</u> (as for example in 之蟲 "these insects") and <u>Leu-shyh Chuen-chiou</u> (as, for example, 之子 "such a person's children," and 之二國者 "these two states," <u>LSCC</u> VI.5 and XVI.3, <u>Syh-buh Bey-yaw</u> Ed.) but which also occurs in this sense on the Oracle Bones. (See <u>LAC</u> 6.4.6.2 footnote 18.)

2.4. <u>Collectives and Restrictives</u>

i. Shift in meaning of <u>Farn</u>

<u>Farn</u> 凡, which occurs in LAC as a collective before

nouns in the sense of "all" or before numbers as "the sum total of" (see <u>LAC</u> 2.6.4.5), occurs in Late Han in the extended sense of "all, > commonplace, > ordinary, common." In LAC it is purely collective. <u>Farn min</u> "all of the common people" does occur in <u>Mencius</u> (7.83), and it is perhaps from such contexts that the shift to "everyday, commonplace" occurs. The shift does not seem to have taken place until Han times. An example from the <u>Commentary</u> is 譬若和氏之璧雖與凡王之璧尺寸厚薄適等,其賈豈可同哉. "By way of illustration, the <u>pi</u> of the Ho Family, though of comparable size and thickness with an ordinary jade <u>pi</u>, could hardly be thought equal in value!" (3.116.)

<u>Examples</u>
凡人 "ordinary person" occurs in 5.127 in contrast to 聖人 "sage"; in 6.114 in contrast to 君子 "the princely man"; and in 4.21, 5.66, 6.112, 7.66 (章), etc. 庸人 "ordinary people" occurs in 7.33 (章) and <u>iong</u> compounds with <u>farn</u> in 凡庸之君 "rulers of the ordinary sort" in 7.66. 凡品 "[people of] the ordinary sort" occurs in 8.69 in contrast to 大聖 "great sages" and 凡夫 "ordinary men" in 7.77. <u>Farn</u> occurs as a noun in 卓絕乎凡 "far removed from the common run [of men]" in 7.85 (章).

ii. <u>Dann</u> before Nouns
An innovation in Late Han is the introduction of the restrictive <u>dann</u> 但. <u>Dann</u> has a wide range of distribution (see <u>Aspect</u> section 3.2.iv and v, <u>Polarity</u> section 3.6.ii, <u>Copula</u> section 6.1.ii and <u>Conjunction</u> section 7.1.ii). In syntagma it occurs before nouns in the sense of "only, only a."

SYNTAGMA   11

Examples
徒善 "mere goodness" in Mencius is rendered in the Commentary 但有善心 "merely to have a good heart" (4.73), but in 但重累之數牆翣之飾有異 "only the number of layers, and the decoration of the coffin, were different" (3.4), dann occurs before nouns.

2.5. The Particle of Syntagma
   i. Jee as a marker of Cause
   In Late Han, jee 者, in addition to its syntagmatic function, becomes a marker of causal clauses. Thus, "verbal clause/jee" becomes "the reason why ..."
   Examples
   美之者欲以責之也 "The reason why he addressed him in this formally elegant fashion, was because he intended thereby to administer a rebuke" (8.116). The clause of cause is also introduced by suoo-yii, thus, 孔子所以危於陳蔡之間者其國君臣皆惡 "The reason why Confucius ran into difficulties in Ch'en and Ts'ai was because the princes and ministers of those states were evil" (8.67); other examples occur in 5.57 (twice); 4.36 (twice); 3.22; 2.16; 1.103, etc.

2.6. The Particle of Determination
   i. Blunting of usage
   In LAC, the determinative relationship between two nouns is marked by jy 之 when the relationship is one of membership in a class, or of possession (see LAC 2.62) Attributive determination is unmarked. In Late Han jy occasionally occurs between attribute and noun.
   Examples
   聖之人 "a Sage" (5.24); 汙亂之世 "a depraved and disorderly generation" (8.117); 寶重之器 "valuable

vessels" (2.18); 密細之網 "a fine net" (1.24); 先聖之王 "the former Sage Kings" (1.94). 不賢之人 "an unworthy man" (1.14); 不正之道 "an improper way" (7.78). Other examples are in 2.106 (章), 2.40, 1.67, 3.108, 6.49, 3.116, etc.

Note. For other changes in the use of jy 之 in Late Han see 2.1.i, 2.2.i above, and 5.3.i and ii, and 8.1.i and ii below.

2.7   SYNTAGMA IN SUMMARY

LAC	LATE HAN	
	Changes in usage	Innovations in usage
2.1 吾：我 > 爾：汝 >	我：我之 [吾] 爾：爾之 [汝]	
2.2 其：之	Occasionally blunted	
2.3 斯：此 >	此/是：with possible 此之：是之 (斯 also becomes 則) 其 demonstrative: 其 "other"	
2.4 凡 "all" >	凡 "common"	但 "only a"
2.5 者 (syntagma)	者 (syntagma) 者 (causal)	
2.6 之 generic only	之 generic and attributive	

In syntagma, therefore, the principal shift is away from specialized determinative forms towards the use of jy 之 as an all-purpose determinative particle, following both nouns and attributes, pronouns and demonstratives.

This leads to the obsolescence of certain of the specialized forms of the pronouns and demonstratives of LAC and to semantic shifts, blunted usage, and reduction of role of others. This shift away from specialized forms, towards all-purpose general forms, is a characteristic generally of the Archaic-Han shift, and will be illustrated further later.

CHAPTER 3

THE VERB

The principal changes in Late Han from LAC usage as they concern the verb are:

(i) A reduction in the role played by the negatives before verbs in determining mood; blunting in the use of the modal negatives; the emergence of bu 不 and wu 無 as all-purpose negatives and their restriction in role to negation; the increase in the use of periphrasis to indicate modality and the introduction of new periphrastic modal forms (See 3.1.)

(ii) Important shifts in role and meaning of certain aspectuals and the occurrence of new aspectuals (See 3.2.)

(iii) The resuscitation of the EAC post-verbal particle tzay 在 (See 3.4.v.)

(iv) A reduction in the role of the post-verbal particles in determining voice, with an increase in the resources for, and the use of periphrastic means of indicating voice (See 3.4.)

(v) Obsolescence of certain polar forms and the introduction of a new one (See 3.6.)

3.1. Mood
   i. The reduction of the role of the Modal
      Negatives to negation

The negatives in LAC play the chief role in determining the mood of the verb (see LAC 3.3.1). They distinguish between the indicative (不) and non-indicative moods (injunctive 毋 subjunctive 無). Two of these modal negatives have a stressed form (indicative 弗 and injunctive 勿), and the indicative has also a form (未) which denies experience of, rather than instances of an act.

THE VERB   15

In Late Han the tendency is towards indicating modality in the verb by periphrastic means and for the negatives to be restricted in function to negation only. This is shown by (i), a tendency to replace the negatives of LAC with bu 不.-- Bu thus becomes a general-purpose negative without modal connotation; and (ii), a tendency to create negated modal forms by using bu in compound forms.

Examples
Examples of LAC negatives replaced with bu:
LAC 弗 is replaced by 不 in 8.27, 8.90; 6.114, 6.125, 7.8, 5.13, 4.125, 6.112, 2.22.[1]
LAC 未 is replaced by 不 in 3.48, 3.110, 2.8.
LAC 無 is replaced by 不 in 3.79, 1.27, 1.107, 3.7.
LAC 否 is replaced by 不 in 5.123, 5.110.
LAC 勿 is replaced by 不 in 1.15, 2.56.
LAC 非 is replaced by 不 in 1.72, 6.77.
Examples of bu 不 in negated compound modal forms are 不須 6.28; 不當 2.90, 2.55; 不得 2.82, 5.10 etc.

Note. Yeou 有 "to occur, or to have," however, is negated with wu 無. Wu ceases to have modal connotations here and has simply the role of "negation before yeou." Examples are 無復有 "will no longer have" (7.77); Wey-yeou 未有 occurs in the Commentary as in the Text in 2.81, 2.82, but is rendered wu-yu 無有 in 2.82 and wu 無 in 1.71 and 1.11; Wu-yu "There was not" occurs in 2.51, 1.113, 1.100.

---

[1] Fwu 弗 is consistently replaced by bu 不 in the Commentary (20 occurrences), except where it is replaced by bu deei 不得 (1.98 (twice) and 8.40) and by bu-keen 不肯 (6.112); Fwu occurs once only in the Commentary (4.97). It is clearly obsolescent in Late Han.

ii. The blunting of the Modal Negatives

One consequence of the reduction of the grammatical role of the negatives is the occurrence of the modal negatives of LAC in blunted and imprecise usage.

Examples
勿 is used for LAC 無 in 7.37.
勿 is used for LAC 不 in 4.83 (章).
莫 is used for LAC 無 in 5.116 (章); 5.80 (章).
莫 is used for LAC 不 in 6.115; 6.117 (章).
未 is used for LAC 不 in 5.20; 6.117 (章); 7.22; 7.26; 7.17; (章); 1.94.
無 is used for LAC 非 in 3.39 (章).[2]

Another consequence is that the modal negatives of LAC are expanded to make clear their modality.

Examples
無 becomes 無可 in 8.117 and 不得 in 2.22; 7.37
勿 becomes 不可以 in 1.28, 不可 in 2.29, and 可無 in 1.106.

iii. Stressed or Intensive Negatives are replaced by periphrastic forms

Stressing and intensification of the negatives, for which special forms are used in LAC (see LAC 3.3.1.1 and 2), tends, in Late Han, to be achieved by periphrastic means. LAC has jong-bu 終不 but Late Han introduces jinq-bu 竟不 ; bih-bu 必不 ; and shu-wu 殊無 in sense of "absolutely not, never on any account, certainly not" etc.

---

[2] It will be seen that most examples of the blunted use of LAC negatives occur in the Chapter Summaries where their use is intended to give an archaic effect. This is typical of Late Han Classical Chinese. See Appendix II.

Examples

今竟不能有燕 "Now, he never could possess Yen" (3.14); 必不受之 "He would on no account accept it" (*bih-bu* here replaces *fwu* 弗 in the Text) (8.18); 殊無所問 "there was absolutely nothing to ask about" (1.48).

iv. Modification in meaning of *Wey*

While the negative *wey* 未 which denies experience of, rather than instances of an act in LAC (see LAC 3.3.1.1) occurs in Late Han, it is sometimes replaced by *bu* 不 (for examples see section 3.1.i above). It occurs typically in Late Han in the narrower sense of "not yet, not so far," and, in this sense, also occurs before numerals.

Examples

未成人 "not yet attained manhood" (4.26); 上世未制禮之時 "in past generations at a time when the Rites had not yet been formulated" (3.122); 未來仕齊也 "not yet come to be employed in Ch'i" - i.e. "before he was employed in Ch'i" (3.20); 己仁恩之未至 "His own imperfect realization of Humanity and kindness" (lit: Humanity/kindness's/not-yet/perfect) (2.104); 孺子未有知小子也 "Ru-tzyy 'baby' is a child before it is aware of things" (lit: not-yet-have knowledge) (2.96); 未葬 (lit: "not-yet buried") > "prior to the burial" (3.55); 未四十 "not yet forty" (2.50).

Note 1. In the last two examples *wey* is used, as *bu-jyi* 不及 or *bih* 比 are used in LAC.[3] 未及 occurs in 未及解稅祭之冕而行 "He left, (even) before he had removed his sacrificial cap" (7.30) but in the Chapter Summary this becomes 冕不及稅 (7.33 (章)).

---

[3] See footnote 2.2.i.

18   LATE HAN CHINESE

<u>Note 2</u>. The reduction in the roles of the negatives in Late Han, and the blurring of the distinctions made by the modal negatives of LAC, are also accompanied by the obsolescence of an LAC feature, whereby polarity is expressed by shifting substitutes (pronouns and demonstratives) from the post-verbal to the pre-verbal position when negated, for which see section 3.6.i below.

v. The blunting of the modal role of <u>Guoo</u> and <u>Guh</u>

In LAC, mood in the verb when unnegated is unmarked. When, however, a change of mood takes place, the <u>zero</u> in <u>zero/verb</u> may be replaced by positive replacements. In the indicative, the positive replacements are <u>guh</u> 固 and <u>guoo</u> 果 (see LAC 3.3.1.4).

In Late Han this purely modal function of <u>guh</u> and <u>guoo</u> is lost, leading to the replacement of <u>gu</u> by <u>suh</u> 素 "as of old" (an innovation in Late Han), and by <u>charng</u> 常 "as always," and to the glossing of <u>guoo</u> by <u>neng</u> 能 "able to" and <u>you jinq</u> 猶竟 "like <u>jinq</u> ('in the end')." <u>Guh</u> and <u>Guoo</u> are then used in these non-modal senses.

<u>Examples</u>

<u>Guh</u> is replaced by 常 in 3.119.
<u>Guh</u> is replaced by 素 in 2.17.
<u>Suh</u> "habitual, habitually, as formerly, formerly," occurs in 5.86; 6.67; 4.24 (章); 7.60.
<u>Guh</u> "really" 3.37; 3.21 (before noun); 2.122.
<u>Guh</u> is used for "as of old, habitually" in 8.54.
<u>Guh</u> is used for "former, formerly," in 4.2.
<u>Guoo</u> is glossed by <u>neng</u> "able to" in 5.66; 5.17; 2.33; 2.122.
<u>Guoo</u> is glossed by <u>you jinq</u>, "rather like saying 'in the end'" in 6.77.

Guoo is used in 果毅 guoo-yih "of fixed purpose" in 2.128.

Note. 固故古 seem quite unstable in Late Han. Guh 故 "therefore" is used for 古 "old" in 故舊 "old friends" (8.111; 8.38) and in 舊故 for "ancient" in 舊故文章 "ancient documents" (4.73). In 2.3 the gloss 故者舊也 occurs. Guh 固 is used for guh 故 "therefore" in 4.107 (章) and in military usage for "strongpoint, defences" in 2.113 and 2.116. This may explain why Jaw Chyi often reads modal guh as suh "habitually, as of old," and as charng "as always." Guoo being glossed as neng 能 "able to" may result from some resemblance between guoo 果 and EAC keh "able to" (Karlgren *Klwâr and *K'ək). (See the Jenq-yih s.v. in 2.33 where Jiau Shyun notes that the Late Han scholar Wei Jau reads 果克也).

vi. The replacement of Yeou and Wei in the Subjunctive

The positive replacements for the subjunctive mood in LAC are 有 for 無 and 為 for 不為 (See LAC 3.3.1.3). Late Han tends to avoid these altogether. A curious replacement for modal yeou "should, ought" is the word guey 貴 "noble" used putatively and injunctively "should give honour to," as for example in 君子有不戰, 戰必勝矣 "a gentleman should not fight, but if he fights, then inevitably he wins" which is translated 君子之道, 貴不戰耳; "In the code of gentlemen it is thought honourable not to fight" (2.116), but which the Ch'ing scholar, Jiau Shyun (loc. cit.) renders 有不戰不當戰也. This same replacement occurs in 朋友有信 "friends should trust [each other]" which is translated as 朋友貴信 "friends should regard with honour the trust they have in each other" (3.104).

Examples

<u>Guey</u> occurs in parallel with <u>bih</u> in 人必趨命貴受其正 "Man must pursue his fated course, and should honourably accept his proper fate" (7.73 (章)); compare also 貴令後世可繼續而行耳 : "[The prince] should [so rule] as to make possible the continuance of his works by his descendants" (2.24) (<u>Text</u> here has 為可繼也); and 學尚虛己師誨貴平. "In learning [a prince] must humble himself. When the teacher instructs, he should be treated as an equal" (8.38 (章)). Conversely, <u>yeou</u> 有 is used for <u>guey</u> in 自有獻子之家 "though they honoured the House of Hsien-tzu" (6.21).

<u>Note</u>. For Ancient Chinese, Karlgren reconstructs 為 *jwie, 貴 *kjwei, 有 *jiəu.

vii. The marking of the Injunctive

The positive replacements for the injunctive and hortatory negatives in LAC are <u>dang</u> 當 and <u>deei</u> 得 (see <u>LAC</u> 3.3.1.4). Both occur in Late Han, but <u>dang</u> occurs with such markedly increased frequency that it is possible that by Late Han the injunctive mood is marked, whether a change of mood takes place or not. <u>Dang</u> and <u>deei</u> are negated with <u>bu</u>.

Examples

(a) <u>Dang</u> occurs in the <u>Commentary</u> where mood is unmarked in the <u>Text</u>. 4.22, 2.134, 2.120, 2.122, 2.116, 2.104, 2.90 (twice), 1.104, 3.86, 3.63, 3.92, 8.103 etc.

(b) <u>Dang</u> is negated with <u>bu</u> 2.90, 2.55, 2.68 etc.

(c) <u>Deei</u> is negated with <u>bu</u> 1.24 (twice), 2.8 (章), 2.82, 5.10.

Note 1. In LAC shanq 尚 occurs in an injunctive sense in Tzuoo Juann (see LAC 3.3.1.2). Shanq occurs in the Chapter Summaries in 學尚虛己 "in learning one should humble oneself" (8.38) (but on this see Appendix 2). Shanq-dang occurs in the Commentary, however, in 尚當問王道 "and so he should have asked about the Way of True Kingship" (1.48).

Note 2. Dang also occurs as a verb "assume responsibility for, take office as, be equal to or adequate for" etc. Examples are 自謂能當名世之子 "he himself said [or thought that] he could fulfil the role of a "scholar famous in his generation" (3.37); 猶當王者 "Even so, one who has assumed the responsibility of Kingship ..." (3.12); 何為當勸齊伐燕乎 "Why would I have assumed the authority to advocate that Ch'i should attack Yen?" (3.12); see also section 7.2.iv below.

viii. The use of Shiu and Ing

Late Han has injunctive and hortatory modals unknown to LAC. One occurring with high frequency is shiu 須 "ought, should." It is negated with bu.

Examples
Shiu occurs before the verb in an injunctive sense in 4.72; 4.112; 4.19; 4.89 (章); etc. Shiu occurs as verb in sense of "should have or be" in 8.66 (章); 7.84; 4.74; 4.79 (章); 4.80; 4.65; 5.81. Shiu is intensified by bih 必 in bih-shiu "must have or be" in 4.64; 2.10; 3.13 (章); 4.84 (章); Shiu is negated with bu in 6.28.

Ing 應 "to reply," "to match up with" has, in part, semantic affinities with dang 當 "to match up to, to correspond to." Ing also occurs, as does dang in an injunctive sense.

Examples

是應得其理也 "and so one must get its principle right" (8.54 (章)); 應法而去 "must go forth in accordance with the laws" (1.97). 虛則不應 "If the reality is lacking, then it does not match up" (8.28章).

Note 1. Bih 必 occurs before verbs in Late Han in the sense of "decidedly, inevitably, of a certainty" etc., for example 必亡 "will certainly be lost" (4.77); 必醉 "will assuredly become drunk" (4.82); 必欲行其道 "will inevitably want to put his way into practice" (2.108) etc. Bih is negated with wey in 未必同也 "is not necessarily the same" (7.26), with bu in 不必知 "did not necessarily know ..." (3.17), and 不必留此學也 "did not need to stay here, to study" (7.11), and with 非 in 庸言必信,非必欲以正行為名也性不忍欺人也 "his every word can certainly be relied upon, not necessarily because he wants to gain a good reputation thereby, but because, by nature, he cannot bear to deceive others" (8.99). Bih occurs before bu (for which see section 3.1.iii above). Bih intensifies shiu 須 in sense of "must have a, must be a" (see 4.64; 2.10; 3.13章), and combines with dang in 當必造朝也 "must certainly go to Court" (2.120). Bih is itself injunctive in 國必修政君必行仁 "the State must cultivate good government, the prince must practice Humanity" (2.89章); see also 1.91 (章), 1.96; etc.

Note 2. Yi 宜 "proper", is used putatively and in hortatory sense "should properly" "properly speaking" and thus, like guey 貴 (see 3.1.vi), has an injunctive and hortatory function. It occurs in 君命宜敬當必造朝 "a prince's summons should be respected, you must certainly go to Court" (2.120). 宜無以錯於廉恥之心 "There should not be that which runs counter to the conscientious heart" (7.78). In this sense dictionaries equate yi with dang 當 and ing 應 (see Tsyr Hae s.v. dang and yi).

ix. The modal functions of Kee and Neng

Dang, deei, shiu, and ing in their negated forms and kee "permitted to, might, could, can" and neng "able to, can" in a negated form tend to replace the injunctive negatives of LAC, or to supplement them, while the positive form takes a double negative, viz. bu kee bu 不可不 and bu neng bu 不能不.

3.2. Aspect

i. Shifts in Potential and Momentary Aspect

Some important functional and semantic shifts occur in the aspectual determinations of the verb in Late Han. LAC chiee 且, potential aspect, "about to" shifts in Late Han to momentary aspect, "for the time being" or "at this moment." LAC yuh 欲 desiderative aspect, "wish to" shifts in Late Han to potential aspect, "about to" "going to."

Examples

Gu 姑 "for the time being" is glossed by chiee 且 in 2.9 and 2.76. Chiee "for time being" occurs in 且使輕之 "let me lighten [taxes] for the time being" (4.39); in 且宿留 "so I stayed for the time being" (3.38); and see also 8.30. Chiee "at that or this moment" occurs in 2.88. Chiee "for a moment" occurs in 且坐 "sit down for a moment" (3.29). Chiee also occurs in the older sense of "about to" in 6.30; and compounded as chiee-yuh 且欲 for "about to" in 3.119. Yuh occurs as potential in 欲如何說之 "How are you going to remonstrate with them?" (7.19) and in 欲絕 "about to break off" (8.73) — see also 3.27; 將欲 occurs in 1.61 for potential aspect.

Fang 方 momentary aspect "at that or this moment" occurs in Late Han in 5.62 and 5.87, which, with chiee, gives fang-chiee 方且 "at this moment," "just on the point of," in 3.29. Jann 暫, momentary aspect, "for the time being," occurs as an innovation in Late Han, replacing jah 乍 "this/that moment" in 2.96, and occurs also in 2.111.

Note. In Han times, yi-chieh is used in the sense of "momentary" as in 以徼一切之勝 "in order to seize a momentary advantage" (How Hann Shu, Wang Bor Juann) or, "interim or emergency" as in 一切增賦 "an interim increase in taxes" (Hann Shu, Dyi Fang-Jinn Juann). Yi-chieh occurs in the Commentary in this sense in 取為一切可勝敵 "They seek for possible momentary advantages over the enemy" (7.78). (This meaning is very well discussed by Jiau Shyun in the Jenq-yih, loc. cit.) In Modern Standard Chinese yi-chieh means "entirely, the whole." It would be of interest to know when the shift of yi-chieh, "momentary" > "the entire, the whole" takes place.

ii. Perfective Aspect

For perfective aspect LAC has jih 既 and yii 已. Late Han prefers yii, replacing jih in the Text by yii. Jih occurs in Late Han in a different usage, in which yii does not occur (for which see section 5.1.ii below).

Examples

Jih is glossed by yii 既已也 (2.139) and replaces jih in 8.62 (2 occurrences); 1.22 etc. Yii occurs in 已下 "already descended" (5.82); 已正 "already rectified" (4.83); 已見 "already appeared in" (4.83); 已美 "already splendid" (7.85); 已説 "already explained" (8.51); 已盛 "already flourishing" (1.43); 已足 "adequate already" (2.46); 已定 "already settled" (2.49.)

THE VERB

iii. The use of <u>Fuh</u> for Durative and
    Iterative Aspect

An important aspectual shift introduces an innovation in Late Han - <u>fuh</u>復. <u>Fuh</u> frequently replaces <u>yow</u>又 not only in its aspectual function "once again" (see <u>LAC</u> 3.3.2.8.a), but also as a conjunction "and too" (for which see section 7.1.i below). But <u>fuh</u> also occurs in Late Han for durative aspect and functions like LAC <u>you</u> (猶) (see <u>LAC</u> 3.3.2.4). <u>Fuh</u> occurs with such high frequency in Late Han, occasionally parasitically, that it might be considered peculiarly characteristic of Late Han. Yoshikawa Kōjirō observes that, later, in Six Dynasties' usage, <u>fuh</u> has "almost no significance."[4]

In its aspectual role, <u>fuh</u> occurs both negated and unnegated, marking durative or continuative aspect. Negated it occurs in sense of "not any longer," "not any further," "not any more." Unnegated it occurs in sense of "continue to, still." <u>Fuh</u> also occurs marking iterative aspect as in LAC in the sense of "once again, again," often in contexts where English has a verb with the prefix re-, as for example 欲復搏之 "intending to recapture it" (8.76).

Examples

(a) Durative Aspect, negated. 不復食羊棗 "he did not eat dates any more" (8.105); 不復為路 "no longer a road" (8.70); 心欲去，故不復受祿 "but in his heart he wanted to leave, and so did not accept a salary any more" (3.38). See also 6.8; 6.47; 4.116; 8.79.

(b) Durative Aspect, not negated. 豈可復謂之外也 "it surely cannot be, that it can still be said to be

---

[4] Yoshikawa Kōjirō "SHIH-SHUO HSIN-YÜ and Six Dynasties Prose Style", <u>HJAS</u> 18 (1955), p. 131.

external" (6.79); 豈可復殘傷其形體 "it surely cannot be, that he can continue to do harm to his body?" (6.64); 富貴而復有德 "rich and highly placed yet still possessed of virtue" (6.21); see also 6.57; 6.47; 3.43; 1.19; etc.

(c) Iterative Aspect

復貢之 "offered him again" (7.25); 復往求見 "went again seeking an interview" (Text has 又) (3.119); 復行古法 "put into practice again the ancient ways" (1.107). See also 5.114; 7.77; 8.76; 8.79; 3.115; 3.124; etc.

(d) Fuh occurs as a verb in, for example, 4.39 "revive" and in 3.77 "restore"; as "anew, newly" in 新復 (3.70); and as "a further" before numerals as in 復三年 "after a further three years" (3.111). Fuh, however, appears to be tautologous and hence parasitic in 復申 "to repeat" (1.12; 1.19; 1.59 etc.) and in 復歸 which is not "to return again" but merely "to return" (8.1).

iv. Dann and Aspect

A further important innovation of Late Han is the introduction of the restrictive dann 但. It is of very frequent occurrence, and, like fuh, might be considered in its frequency to be peculiarly characteristic of Late Han. Determining the verb in the aspectual position, dann occurs as "merely, only," and is comparable with dan 單 in LAC.

Examples

凡人但不能演用為行耳 "the ordinary person merely cannot apply them in practice" (2.97); 但有爵耳 "He merely possesses a noble title" (2.123); 但治其爭訟 "only settled their disputes" (3.25); 人君但養犬彘 "Rulers merely provide food for their dogs and pigs" (1.30); 水豈無分於上下乎, 水性但欲下耳, "It surely cannot be that water cannot differentiate between upwards and downwards! Water, by nature, merely wishes to flow downwards!" (6.66). 不但坐而聽命 "He does not merely sit awaiting the dictates of fate" (8.79). Other examples will be found in 7.24; 7.45; 7.27; 7.8; 6.24; 6.44; etc.

v. *Dann* and Polarity

But *dann* is of such frequent occurrence in Late Han, and the restrictive aspect of comparatively rare occurrence in LAC, that it is difficult to dismiss all occurrences of *dann* before verbs as purely aspectual. *Dann* is often in comparable distribution with *bu* 不, as, for example, 但言...不言... "he merely said ... he did not say ..." (2.74); 但聞...不聞... "I have only heard that ... I have not heard that ..." (2.8); 但加載書不復歃血 "He merely attached the document [to the sacrifice] but did not, also, smear the blood on the lips [of those swearing the oath]" (7.37); 但食之而不愛 "... merely to feed him but not to love him ..." (8.27); 人君但崇庖廚養犬馬不恤民 "Princes merely devote their attention to their kitchens and to the care of their horses and hounds, but they do not shew compassion for the common people" (4.50); 不勸王使我得行道, 而但勸我畱 "You did not advocate that the King should allow me to put my Way into practice, but merely advocated that I should be detained" (3.30). Other examples will be found in 8.27; 2.92; 2.125; etc.

Here, *dann* is functioning in a way reminiscent of *wei* 惟 in its polarity with *fei* 非 in EAC (see *EAC* 4.8). Looked at from the point of view of its polarity with *bu*, *dann* might be thought of as of a class with the negatives, as a sort of partial or restricted negation. <u>Dann</u> here, as it were, anticipates a total negation. Whether expressed (with a <u>bu</u> clause) or not, <u>dann</u> involves an antithesis.

Unnegated <u>dann</u> anticipates a negative antithesis. Negated, as for example in 不但坐而聽命 "He does not merely sit awaiting the dictates of fate" (8.79), <u>dann</u> anticipates a positive antithesis. In this instance it is supplied in the context. 聖人亹亹不倦,不但坐而聽命故曰君子不謂命也 "The Sage is indefatigable, never tiring. He does not merely sit awaiting the dictates of fate. That is why it is said 'the True Gentleman [i.e. Confucius] did not discuss fate.' In all the pre-verbal occurrences of <u>dann</u> there is, either directly expressed with a conjunction (<u>erl</u>) or implicit, an adversative.

<u>Note</u>. <u>Dann</u> in Late Han is thus not far removed from the adversative conjunction <u>dann-shyh</u> 但是 "but" or <u>dann-tzer</u> 但則 of Modern Standard Chinese, and may possibly, in Late Han, have occurred in this conjunctive sense, as the following examples suggest: 之以為當同其恩愛無有差次等級相殊也.但施愛之事,先從己親屬始耳.若此何為獨非墨道也 "Chih thought that we should shew love and kindness to all equally - that there should not be any discrimination between the degrees of kinship and of rank. But, in the matter of shewing love, that we should begin with our own kinsfolk. If this was so, [Chih thought] why should the Mohists be singled out for censure?" (3.120); and, in his paraphrase of <u>Songs</u> 192 cited in 1.109, Jaw Chyi has 居今之世可矣,富人.但憐憫此煢獨羸弱者耳 "Living in this present age, it is the rich who get by, but pity these, the weak and lonely" (1.109).

These examples are not conclusive, for the first may

well be 但施愛之事. "It is only in the matter of shewing our love that we ..." and the second be "I merely pity these, the weak and lonely." In all the fifty-three occurrences of dann in the Text, these are the only two examples that might even be thought of as conjunctive.

vi. The use of Jyi and Biann
Jyi 即 which occurs in LAC as a copula (see LAC 4.4.2) and as a conditional conjunction (see LAC 5.3), occurs in the aspectual position in Late Han in the sense of "at once, immediately." This usage is an innovation in Late Han.

Examples
不欲即去 "I did not want to leave immediately" (3.38); 知攘之惡當即止 "If you know stealing them to be wrong, you should stop doing it at once" (4.40); 所止舍館未定，故不即來 "The arrangements for the lodgings at which I was to stay were not yet settled and so I did not come at once" (4.122); 舜入而即去,瞽瞍不知其已出 ... "Shun went down into [the well] but came out immediately afterwards. Ku-sou, unaware that he had already come out ..." (5.82). Jaw Chyi's use of jyi leads him to translate 即不忍其觳觫 "It was true that I could not bear to see its shuddering" as 即見其牛哀之 "As soon as I saw that ox, I pitied it" (1.53), thus retaining jyi in his translation but giving it a Late Han meaning.

In similar usage, biann 便 occurs in Late Han as an innovation, seemingly interchangeably with jyi. It occurs in the sense of "at once, immediately, straightaway."

Examples

公何為不便見孟軻 "Why did your grace not see Mencius straight away?" (2.31) (Jiau Shyun, in his _Jenq-yih_ in loc., says "便 is like 利, 利 is like 快. The passage means 其遲滯不即見 "He dallied, not seeing him at once.") 彼不復問孰可, 便自往伐之 "They did not also ask me 'who should [attack Yen]' but, of their own volition, immediately went off and attacked it" (3.12); 陽貨視孔子亡而饋之者, 欲使孔子來答, 恐其便答拜使人也 "The reason why Yang Huo sent a gift of food when he saw that Confucius was not at home was because he wished to make Confucius come to him to return the visit. He was afraid that [if Confucius were at home] he would immediately bow to the messenger [and thus fulfil his obligation to return the visit]" (4.36).

vii. The use of _Meei_ and _Jer_

In LAC _meei_ 每 occurs before the verb in the sense of "on each occasion, each time" (see LAC 3.3.2.8). In Late Han, _che_ 輒, an innovation, fulfils this role, either singly or in combination with _meei_, viz. _meei-jer_ 每輒.

Examples

丑怪孟子不肯每輒應諸侯之聘不見之於義謂何也 "[Kung-sun] Ch'ou was perplexed at Mencius' unwillingness to reply each time to the invitations of the Feudal Lords [and asked] what principle of justice was involved in his not seeing them" (4.34); 不知可繼續而常來致之乎, 將當輒更以君命將之也 "I do not know if he can, time after time, be continually coming and presenting gifts, or if he should bring them, having obtained the prince's order afresh each time?" (6.43); 每人而輒欲自加恩以悅其意, 則日力不足以足

之也 "If each time he wishes to be kind to each and every man that comes in order to please the dictates of his desires, then his daily strength will be insufficient to satisfy their needs" (5.8); 過小耳而孝子感激,輒怨其親,是亦不孝也 "When the faults of the parents are minor ones but the filial son is moved to anger by them, so that each time (they happen) he feels resentment against his parents, then this, too, is to be unfilial" (7.15).

3.3. Manner
　i. The misinterpretation of Yan
　The Commentary twice interprets "verb/yan 焉" as an attribute (either reading yan for ran 然, or as a maw 貌).[5] x-yan, and xx-yan, thus, by Late Han times, are interpreted as x-ran or xx-ran. (See also Section 5.3.ii below.)

　Examples
　Text 心有戚戚焉 "in my mind, there was a sense of familiarity with it (i.e. with what you said"). Commentary 戚戚然,心有動也 "chi-chi-ran means as when the mind is stirred" (1.55); Text 眸子眊焉 "The pupil of the eye is dulled by it"; Commentary 眊者蒙蒙目不明之貌 "Mau means 'as though blindfold, the eye not seeing'" (4.108). Neither occurrence gives a materially false interpretation of the Text but yan is given the value ran and not of yu jy, as, properly, it should be given in Mencius.

---

[5] For maw see Appendix 4.

ii. The interpretation of 'yeou/attribute' and 'attribute/sy'

The occurrence of attribute/sy 斯, and yeou 有/attribute in the Book of Songs is commonly interpreted by Han writers as a reduplication of the attribute.[6] This influences Jaw Chyi's interpretation of Mencius.

Examples
Text 其顙有泚 "His brow broke out in sweat" but the Commentary explains (no doubt influenced by a gloss on 有泚 in the Songs as 鮮明貌, see Jenq-yih in loc.) as 泚 汗出 泚泚然也 "tzyy means "glistening with sweat" (3.123). But, on a citation from the Songs in the Text, 王赫斯怒 "The King flushed in anger," the Commentary has 王赫然斯怒 (1.88).

3.4. Voice

In LAC, the voice of the verb is governed by the disposition of the two post-verbal elements (see LAC 3.4). The positions vis-à-vis each other of these two elements is governed by their relation to the particle of the post-verbal position (in LAC 於 and 乎 and in EAC 于). While, in LAC, these particles do not always occur with predictable regularity, their function, in so far as the voice of the verb is concerned, is decisive. In Late Han there is a perceptible shift towards indicating voice

---

[6] See Wang Shean 王顯 "Shy-jing jong gen chorng-yan tzuoh-yonq shiang-dang-de Yeou-tzyy shyh, Chyi-tzyy shyh, Sy-tzyy shyh, her Sy-tzyy shyh." 詩經中跟重言作用相當的有字式, 其字式, 斯字式, 合思字式 Yeu-yan Yan-jiou 語言研究 4 (1959), pp. 9-43.

THE VERB   33

by periphrastic means and for the post-verbal particles to become simply markers of the locative.

i. The <u>Jiann</u> Passive

The use of <u>jiann</u>見 for the periphrastic passive is of rare occurrence in LAC. In Late Han it is exceedingly common. In addition Late Han introduces three innovations for marking the passive voice, namely, <u>wei</u>為; <u>bey</u>被; and <u>meng</u>蒙.

<u>Examples</u>

In the <u>jiann</u> passive, <u>jiann</u> occurs immediately before the verb. <u>Jiann</u> occurs twice and <u>wei</u> once in the following translation of an LAC original which has no passive voice at all. 言為人所悅將見禪為天子皆不足以解憂獨見愛於父母為可以解己之憂 "It means, delighted in by others and about to be placed in the succession for the Throne - neither of these two things was sufficient to dispel his [Shun's] grief. Being loved by his parents, by that alone could he have dispelled his grief" (5.77). The positional passive of the <u>Text</u> is replaced by the periphrastic passive in 不悅於魯衛 which becomes 不見悅魯衛之君 "disliked by the rulers of Lu and Wei" (5.125), and an unmarked passive is replaced by the periphrastic passive in 以貨取乎 which becomes 以貨財見取乎 "[When has a True Gentleman been] procured with a bribe?" (2.128). Other examples are 見愛 "beloved" (8.116); 見薄 "shabbily treated" (8.39); 見惡 "hated" (5.72); 見放 "exiled" (5.93); 見稱 "designated" (5.127); 不見用 "unemployed" (6.34); 見削奪 "be encroached upon" (7.26); 見貢 "be offered up" (7.25); 見亡 "be destroyed" (4.89); 不見知 "be unknown" (5.70); 見侮慢 "be treated with discourtesy" (4.92); 見浸 "be invaded" (2.88) etc.

ii. The Bey Passive

A metaphorical extension of the verb bey 被 "to wear, to cover" and thus > "to be under the effect of" > "be affected by," "to suffer," produces, when occurring before another verb, a periphrastic passive.

Examples
Bey "to wear," "be clothed by" occurs in 則天下被覆衣之仁也, "then the world will be clothed in the covering-cloak of Humanity" [literally "covering-cloak-Humanity"] (4.74). (The Text puts this in the active voice 仁覆天下 "Humanity covers over the world.") "Affected by" occurs in 使百姓被澤 "so as to allow the people to be affected by its refreshing dews [i.e. its beneficence]" (4.72). See also 被恩 "affected by kindness" (8.45 (章)); Bey occurs as "suffer" as in 被病 "suffering from sickness" (6.87) and 被其害 "suffer harm" (8.44). But in the following bey, almost devoid of semantic content, merely marks the passive 常常被服 "forever controlled (by it)" (8.71 (章)).

Note. Meng 蒙 "to receive, meet with, etc." is comparable to bey in 被其害 "suffer harm" (8.44) in a proverb cited in the Commentary 鳶鵲蒙害仁鳥曾逝 "When kites and magpies suffer harm the kindly [?edible] birds fly high" (5.12); Meng also occurs in 蒙其恥辱 "be regarded with contempt by them" (2.85).

iii. The Periphrastic Passive in <u>Wei</u>

In the distribution "<u>wei</u> 為/active agent/<u>suoo</u> 所/verb" the verb is passive, but the "<u>wei</u> α <u>suoo</u> β" matrix itself is a syntagma and occurs only as a unit in sentences.

<u>Examples</u>
(a) wei   X   Y
不為俗移 "not shifted by fashion" (7.84) (章)
(b) wei   X suoo Y
為知者所笑 "laughed at by those who know" (8.76); 為眾口所詬 "reviled by everyone" (8.67); 為楚所滅 "destroyed by Ch'u" (5.125); 為曾西所羞 "despised by Tseng Hsi" (2.48) (章).
(c) Examples of positional passive in the <u>Text</u> translated in the <u>Commentary</u> by the <u>wei</u> passive. <u>Text</u>: 而蔽於物 <u>Commentary</u>: 為物所蔽 "and so are impinged upon by objects" (6.122); <u>Text</u>: 終身不養 <u>Commentary</u>: 終身不為妻子所養也 "for the rest of his life he was not looked after by his wife and children" (5.61).

<u>Note</u>. The <u>jiann</u>, <u>wei</u> and <u>bey</u> passive forms occur, each in a distinctive form of distribution. This is best shown in tabular form.

	Pre-verbal	Verb	Post-verbal
Either	以 [noun]	見 /verb	[or noun]
		被 [noun]	[or verb]
	為 [noun]	所 /verb	

The <u>noun</u> in parenthesis is in each case the instrumentality through which the agent suffers the action of the verb, and, as will be seen, is in contrastive distribution in all three forms of the periphrastic passive. In the case of <u>jiann</u> this instrumentality occurs post-verbally in 不見悅魯衛之君... "disliked by the rulers of Lu and Wei" (5.125) and pre-verbally in the instrumental position in 以貨財見取乎 "procured with a bribe!" (2.128). In the case of <u>bey</u> the instrumentality occurs immediately after <u>bey</u> as in 亦并被其害 "and both are harmed by it" (8.44), where <u>chyi hay</u> is nominal, "suffered its harmfulness," but in examples like 被服 "controlled by it" (8.71), <u>bey</u> occurs before a verb. (A not dissimilar possibility occurs in Modern Standard Chinese, viz. 欺他 <u>chi-ta</u> "cheat him" 他被欺了 <u>ta bey chi-le</u> "he was cheated," 被了他的欺 <u>bey-le ta-de chi</u> "cheated by him!") In the case of <u>wei</u>, <u>wei</u> introduces the instrumentality, and <u>suoo</u> (when occurring) marks the verb.

iv. Causative and permissive

The periphrastic causative in LAC is formed with <u>shyy</u> 使 (see LAC 3.4.5). Late Han uses <u>shyy</u> but also introduces <u>linq</u> 令, which is interchangeable with <u>shyy</u>. The periphrastic causative is of much more frequent occurrence in Late Han. <u>Shyy</u> and <u>linq</u> also occur in Late Han in an extended sense, from "cause, bring about, make" to "permit, let, allow."

Examples
Examples of the permissive use of <u>shyy</u> and <u>linq</u> 皆不欲使世子行三年 "None of them wanted to allow the Heir Apparent to serve the three year mourning period" (3.49); 且無令士親肌膚 "further, not to let the earth come into close contact with the body" (3.7).

Note. <u>Ting</u> "to listen, to obey" occurs in Late Han in an extended sense, as "to let or to allow." Examples are 文王聽民往取禽獸 "King Wen allowed his people to go into [his park] and take game" (1.82). 告則不聽其娶 "if he had told them, they would not have allowed him to marry" (5.81). 說以方且聽子為政 "they explained that [the King] was just about to allow the Master [i.e. Tzu-ssu] to take charge of the government" (3.29).

v. *Tzay* as a post-verbal particle

The particles of the post-verbal position of LAC are yu 於 and hu 乎 (see LAC 3.4) and of EAC, yu 于 (see EAC 3.4). Hu 乎 and yu 于 are obsolescent in Late Han and are replaced by yu 於. Yu 於, however, is occasionally replaced by tzay 在 or occurs in combination with tzay, i.e. tzay-yu 在於.[7] The tendency in Late Han is for these particles to become simply markers of the locative and for their role in the indication of voice in LAC to be supplanted by the periphrastic means already described. Yu 於 occurring in the Text is sometimes disregarded altogether in the Commentary.

Examples
於 is replaced by tzay-yu in 2.99;
乎 is replaced by yu in 4.85, 8.117, 5.25;
乎 is replaced by tzay in 4.108;
於 is replaced by tzay in 4.32, 6.125;
在 is used for yu in 2.65, 5.21, 3.47, 8.120, 2.82.
Yu in the Text is disregarded in 入於井 which becomes 入井 (2.96); 害於天下 which becomes 害之 (2.61); 擇於斯二者 which becomes 擇此二者 (2.29); 快於是 which becomes 快是 (1.61); 造於朝 which becomes 造朝 (2.120.) See also 3.122, where

---

[7] 在 in 在於 in LAC is a verb. It occurs as "verb/post-verbal particle," "to reside in, to lie with, etc." In Late Han 在於 occurs in the collocation "verb/tzay-yu/post-verbal element" and is thus a particle of the post-verbal position.

諸 (=之於) is disregarded in the <u>Text</u> in 有諸內必形諸外 which becomes 有中則見外 "what one possesses inwardly is manifested outwardly" (7.27).

<u>Note</u>. <u>Tzay</u>, in this usage, is not an innovation in Late Han, but the resuscitation of an EAC feature in Late Han (see <u>EAC</u> 3.4.5.1 especially footnote 26). For other resuscitations see sections 4.2.v and 5.1.ii below.

3.5. Direction

i. <u>Tzyh</u> is replaced by <u>Tsorng</u>

When direction is treated periphrastically, LAC <u>tzyh</u> 自 "from" is consistently replaced in Late Han by <u>tsorng</u> 從. <u>Tzyh</u> in Late Han usage is used, singly or in combination, for "self" (as reflexive when in the pre-verbal position, and in the agential distributive position in sense of "agent acts in his own interests, or in person" - usually contrary to expectation"). <u>Tzyh</u> is also used in Late Han in a new sense as a form of concession (see section 7.3.i below). This suggests a sort of chiasmus.

```
LAC                          LATE HAN
Tzyh 自 "from"         ⤬     Tsorng 從 "from"
Tzonq 縱 "even if"           Tzyh 自 "even if"
```

Examples

<u>Tzyh</u> is defined as <u>tsorng</u> in 5.110 and 3.73, and <u>tsorng</u> replaces <u>tzyh</u> in 3.4, 3.43, etc. <u>Tzonq</u> occurs as a verb in Late Han, in the sense of "to loosen, let go" (6.87 and 6.105) and as an attribute in "loose living" in 4.25.

<u>Note</u>. The replacement of <u>tzyh</u> "from" by <u>tsorng</u> "from," in Late Han writers, is remarked on by Jiau Shyun who observes that other Late Han scholars, Jenq Shyuan 鄭玄 (127-200 A.D.) in his <u>Notes</u> 箋 on the <u>Book of Songs</u>, and Gau Yow 高誘 (2nd century A.D.) in his <u>Commentaries</u> on the 呂氏春秋 and on the 淮南子 "both take <u>tzyh</u> to be <u>tsorng</u>" (皆以自為從) (<u>Jenq-yih</u> 3.74).

THE VERB

ii. You is replaced by Tsorng

LAC also uses you 由 for the periphrastic treatment of direction. You, like tzyh (see para. i above), is consistently replaced by tsorng 從 and thus is obsolescent in this sense in Late Han.

Examples
You is replaced by tsorng in 2.40, 2.81, 3.120, 6.87, and by yu 於 in 4.42.

Note. You 由 also occurs in LAC used for you 猶 "is like." The Commentary has two occurrences of you in this usage (2.67 and 2.68) but elsewhere replaces you with ru 如, ruoh 若 or pih-you 譬由 (1.44, 2.39, 6.7). You before a verb is modal (as is you 猶) in LAC. This is disregarded in translation (see section 3.1.vi above). The verbal usage of you "to use, to avail oneself of, to pursue [a course] or follow [a road]" occurs indifferently in LAC and Late Han. Late Han, however, uses her-you 何由, not in the sense of "from whence" as in LAC, but in a new sense of "of what use." (See section 8.3.v below.) You is twice defined as 用也 (5.70, 7.76) and this is its main use in Late Han.

3.6. Polarity

i. The obsolescence of the polar form
   'negative/substitute/verb'

LAC has a feature in which a negated verb, particularly when the verb is negated with a stressed negative, drops the pronouns and demonstratives which would occur in the post-verbal position, if the verb were not negated. This feature is unknown to Late Han. In translation, the dropped pronoun is often supplied, and numerous examples occur of negated verbs followed by pronouns and demonstratives. This suggests that between LAC and Late Han a change takes place in the intonational pattern of the sentence though this is impossible to demonstrate. It does, however, provide further evidence of the reduction in the role of the negatives, already referred to in section 3.1.i above.

<u>Examples</u>
"不 /verb/pronoun", occurs in 2.73, 3.20, 3.6, 2.139 (章), 2.77, 5.42, 7.8, 6.117, 6.24, 6.27, 4.125, 4.73 (twice), 2.108, 3.119, 2.124, 8.97, 6.112.
"不 /verb/demonstrative", occurs in 1.29, 5.20, 7.55, 1.61.
"弗 /verb/demonstrative", occurs in 4.97.
"無 /verb/pronoun", occurs in 2.20, 4.22, 6.27, 8.115.
"未 /verb/pronoun", occurs in 2.13.
"勿 /verb/pronoun", occurs in 6.112.

ii. <u>Dann</u> and Polarity

A corollary of the dropping of the polar emphasis of LAC described in the previous paragraph is the occurrence in paired statements of <u>dann</u> 但 with either a negative or positive polar statement, explicit or implied. This has been described already in section 3.2.v above.

3.7.   THE VERB IN SUMMARY

LAC	LATE HAN	
	Changes in usage	Innovations in usage
Mood 不:弗 and 未	Tend to converge on 不 and lose modality. 未 becomes "not yet"	竟不；必不；殊無；for emphatic negation
毋 ； 勿	> Obsolescent - preference for periphrastic forms	
固 ； 果	Lose modality and converge with 能 常 etc.	素 "as of old"
有 ； 為	Use avoided as modals	
當 ； 得	Used with markedly increased frequency.	須；應 "should" "ought" "needs to"
Aspect 且 (potential)	>且 (momentary)	暫；暫且；方且 一切 "momentarily"
欲 (desiderative)	>欲 (potential)	
既；已 (perfective)	>已 (perfective)	
復 (iterative)	>復 (iterative and durative)	

THE VERB IN SUMMARY

LAC	LATE HAN	
	Changes in usage	Innovations in usage
Aspect 單 (restrictive) 每 "each time"		但 (restrictive) 但 (in polar role) 但 (adversative) 輒;每輒 "each time" 即;便 "immediately"
Manner	為 in blunted usage	
Voice 於 (于:乎) 見 (passive) 使 (causative)	>於;在;在於 見 (passive) 為 (passive) 使(causative and permissive) 令 (causative and permissive)	被 (passive) 蒙 (passive) 聽 (permissive)
Direction 自 "from" 縱 "even if" 由 "from"	>從 "from" >自 "even if" >從 "from"	
Polarity Negative/substi- tute/verb	Obsolescent	

The principal shift in the verb and its determinations is away from specialized forms of the negative and towards the use of periphrasis to indicate mood, which, when in the negative, uses an all-purpose negative, *bu*. This leads to the obsolescence of certain of the special modal negative forms of LAC and to the occurrence of new periphrastic forms to indicate modality. Voice, too, tends towards the use of periphrastic means, with the consequent reduction in role of the post-verbal particles, and a tendency away from the strict positional syntax by which voice is imposed in LAC.

The shift away from specialized forms to the use of all-purpose forms, is, as has already been seen in the syntagmatic level (see section 2.7 above), a characteristic of the Archaic-Han Shift. The use of periphrasis is, too, characteristic with a consequent blunting and semantic loss among the "empty words," and together these constitute one of the main features of the Archaic-Han Shift.

CHAPTER 4

AGENCY

The principal changes in Late Han from LAC usage as they concern Agency are:

(i) A preference for the pregnant rather than the determinative forms of the personal pronouns for the Agent (see 4.1).

(ii) The obsolescence of certain specialized agential distributives and the encroachment of jiu 俱 upon jie 皆 and jie 偕 and of shwei 誰 upon shwu 孰. The resuscitation of shyan 咸 (see 4.2).

(iii) The parasitic occurrence of shiang 相 and the obsolescence of jiau 交 for reciprocity (see 4.3).

(iv) Blunted usage in indicating delegated agency (see 4.4).

(v) The restriction of tzyh 自 to the Reflexive (see 4.5).

4.1. The Pronouns

i. Obsolescence of the agentive forms of the Pronouns

In LAC, where the agent is represented by a personal pronoun, the determinative forms wu 吾 (first person) and eel 爾 (second person) occur. In Late Han these are almost totally replaced by the pregnant forms woo 我 and ruu 汝. This tendency is parallel to the tendency already noted (see section 2.1 above) for the determinative pronouns to become assimilated in the pregnant forms, and for the distinction between the determinative and agential form, on the one hand, and the pregnant form on the other, to disappear.

AGENCY   45

The determinative pronouns occur sporadically in the Text in the agential position but never in the post-verbal position. If it were not for this, there would be justification for regarding wu and erl in Late Han as simple stylistic variants of woo and ruu.

Late Han still adheres, however, to the "agential/post-verbal" distinction in the anaphoric pronouns chyi 其 and jy 之 though, as noted in section 2.2 above and elsewhere, blunting and certain semantic shifts occur in the use of the anaphoric pronouns.

Examples
(a) Agential wu is replaced by woo in 1.61, 1.62, 1.66, 1.97, 2.4, 2.134, 3.119, 3.51, 3.52, 3.48, 4.6, 4.51, 6.107, 8.103, etc.
(b) Yu 予 is replaced by woo in 1.18, 2.34, 2.37, 2.127, 2.139, 3.22, 3.33, 4.41, 5.38, 7.66, etc.

4.2. The Distributives
i. The Obsolescence of Huoh 或 and Moh 莫
The agential distributives of LAC -- huoh 或 "of the agents some" and moh 莫 "of the agents none" (for which see LAC 3.5.3.1) -- are obsolete in Late Han as such.

Huoh is consistently paraphrased as yeou 有 or yeou-ren 有人 "there are those who." A possible reason for this is that the function of huoh shifts in Late Han to use as a selective conjunction, in the form huoh ... huoh ... "some ... some ..." > "either ... or ...," developing eventually into a simple selective conjunction "or."

Moh, on the other hand, in common with the other specialized forms of the negatives of LAC, becomes subsumed in wu 無 and bu 不 and loses its distinctively agential role.

Examples

(a) <u>Huoh</u> is defined as 有也 in 2.139, and is replaced by 有; 有人 etc. in 7.23, 5.128, 5.122, 5.91, 8.90, 5.62, 3.11, 8.30, etc.

(b) <u>Huoh</u> repeated, "either ... or ..." 或殀或壽 "whether they die prematurely, or live to a ripe old age" (7.70); 或得或否 "whether he gets it or not" (7.74); 或折或引 "whether by breaking off or leading forth" (7.67 (章)); 或見或否 "whether he saw them or not" (7.24 (章)); 或爲君子或爲小人 "whether he be a princely man or a petty man" (6.101).[1]

(c) <u>Moh</u> defined as <u>wu</u>

<u>Moh</u> is glossed by <u>wu</u> 莫無也 in 5.113 and 7.71.

<u>Moh</u> is replaced by <u>wu</u> in 5.100, 3.61, 8.32, 2.121, 2.102, 3.61, 1.49, etc.

<u>Moh</u> is used like <u>bu</u> in 6.115.

<u>Moh</u> is replaced by <u>chii</u> 豈 in 2.121.

<u>Note</u>. The selective conjunction of LAC is <u>ruoh</u> (see LAC 2.5). <u>Ruoh</u> 若 occurs in the <u>Commentary</u> in reduplicated form, not unlike <u>huoh</u> above. 若遊若豫豫亦遊也 "whether it be called <u>you</u> or <u>yuh</u>, <u>yuh</u> is after all <u>you</u>" (1.96).

---

[1] Janusz Chmielewski in his "Notes on Early Chinese Logic (II)" <u>Rocznik Orientalistyczny</u> XXVI.2 (1963), pp. 91-106, has an interesting discussion of the evolution of this usage of <u>huoh</u>. It was not, as he says, listed in <u>Late Archaic Chinese</u>. This was not an oversight on my part. The 或...或... form does not occur as early as the Late Archaic period.

AGENCY

ii. The encroachment of Jiu upon Jie and Jie

In LAC, the agential distributive jie 皆 "all" and jie 偕 "both" are restricted to the agential position (for which see LAC 3.5.3). In Late Han jie 偕 is obsolescent and is replaced by jiu 俱. Jie 皆, on the other hand, occurs not only as an agential distributive, but as a collective (an innovation in Late Han), functioning (as does jiu 俱) as a determinant via the verb of post-verbal elements; jiu 俱 thus subsumes jie 偕, and attracts jie 皆 into the function jiu performs in Late Han. Jiu 俱 also, and wrongly, replaces jiau 交 for reciprocity for which see section 4.3.i below.

Examples

(a) 俱 replaces 偕. See 1.18 and 2.111 where 偕 is defined as 俱; Jiu occurs in the agential distributive position in sense of "both" in 俱出文王 "both [the T'eng and Lu ducal houses] descended from King Wen" (3.49); 雖俱白 "though both are white (6.68); 俱含天氣 "both [men and animals] breathe the air of Heaven" (5.30 (章)). See also 1.23.

(b) Jie as a collective. Jie 皆 occurs before the verb, determining its post-verbal elements in 人不能皆如其願也 "Man cannot do all that he wishes to do" (8.78); 而皆信之 "and believe all of it" (8.49); 能皆實而無虛 "[if one] can see as true all of it, and as false none, [then] ..." (7.74); 皆錄之於春秋 "recorded them all in the Ch'un Ch'iu" (8.45) 舜...皆取人之善謀而從之 "Shun accepted all good advice tendered by others and complied with it" (2.106); 孟子皆曰否 "Mencius replied with a 'no' to all [three questions]" (7.55).

iii. Jiu as a Collective

Jiu occurs before the verb, determining its post-verbal elements in 俱答二人獨見李子 "He replied to both of the two, but saw only one of them namely Chi Tzu" (7.22). 俱有好憎 "has both likes and dislikes" (6.101); 俱賢之 "thought both of them worthy" (5.57).

iv. Shwu is assimilated into Shwei

Shwu 孰 which in LAC usage is restricted to the agential distributive position and is an interrogative substitute ("of the agents which one"?) (see LAC 6.5.2.4) is replaced by shwei 誰 "who"? in Late Han. Where shwu occurs in Late Han, seemingly as a stylistic variant for shwei, it is used in a blunted sense.

Examples

Shwu is replaced by shwei in 8.16, 5.106, 3.12, 3.24, 1.42. Jaw Chyi transposes 膾炙與羊棗孰美, "Cooked meat or dates -- which of the two is the better [eating]?" to 羊棗孰與膾炙美也 "who thinks dates are better than cooked meats to eat?" (8.105); Shwu is replaced by her-wey in 問二者何為重 "He asked of the two what was the more important" (Text has 禮與食孰重 "The Rites [observed when eating] and eating [itself], which is the more important?" (7.1).)

v. The use of Shyan

Shyan 咸 which occurs commonly in EAC (see EAC 3.5.3) and sporadically in LAC (mainly in citation) occurs in Late Han.

Examples

使無罪者咸恐懼也 "makes all the innocent fearful" (8.39); 咸以仁義相接 "all conducting their inter-relationships according to Humanity and Justice" (7.21); 咸願以為師 "all want to make [them] their teachers" (1.2).

<u>Note</u>. See also 3.4.v and 5.1.ii for other resuscitations of EAC forms in Late Han.

4.3. <u>Reciprocity</u>
   i. The obsolescence of <u>Jiau</u> and the parasitic use of Shiang

In LAC, <u>shiang</u> 相 and <u>jiau</u> 交 (and also the compound form <u>jiau-shiang</u> 交相) occur before the verb to indicate reciprocity of action in the agents. (See <u>LAC</u> 3.5.4.) <u>Shiang</u> occurs in this role in Late Han, but <u>Jiau</u> is obsolescent. <u>Shiang</u> also occurs, parasitically, before certain verbs, where no reciprocity is intended.

<u>Examples</u>
Parasitic <u>shiang</u>: 不相欺惑小 "no cheating of the young and innocent" (3.115); 不相與言 "does not talk to them" (2.139 (章)); 不足以相笑也是人俱走 "They are in no position to laugh at the others, because both groups ran away" (1.23).

<u>Note</u>. In 1.6 <u>jiau</u> occurs in the <u>Text</u> in the sense of "reciprocity" and is so read by <u>Jiau Shyun</u> (交互之交). Jaw Chyi has as comment 交爭各欲利其身, and says that another explanation is to read <u>jiau</u> as 俱. Jiau Shyun observes in this latter connection that both Gau Yow 高誘 in his <u>Commentary</u> on the <u>Jann-gwo Tseh</u> and <u>Wei Jau</u> 韋昭 in his <u>Commentary</u> on the <u>Gwo-yeu</u> read 交 as 俱. Both are Late Han writers. This suggests that in Late Han <u>jiau</u> for reciprocity is not only obsolescent, but has been wrongly assimilated with the collective 俱.

4.4. Delegated Agency

i. <u>Wey</u> encroaches upon <u>Wey</u>

Where one agent is said to act for, or in the interests of another, <u>wey</u> 為 introduces the second agent (see LAC 3.5.5). In Late Han <u>wey</u> is occasionally assimilated with <u>wey</u> 謂, particularly in those contexts where <u>wey</u> occurs in <u>yii-wey</u> (以為) constructions. <u>Wey</u> 謂 then occurs, marking "delegated agency."

<u>Examples</u>
(a) 以為 becomes 謂
<u>Text</u> 百姓皆以王為愛也 "The people thought the King was mean" becomes 百姓皆謂王嗇愛其財, "The people thought the King miserly with his wealth" (1.52); <u>Text</u> 於予心猶以為速 "I myself thought that [my departure] was all too fast" becomes 我自謂行速疾矣, "I myself thought my going very fast" (3.32); 謂孟子欲自比孔子 "thinking that Mencius wished to compare himself with Confucius" (2.74); 小人苟得謂不見知 "petty people gain it by means that are wrong, thinking that it will not be known" (5.70 (章)). Other examples are in 1.53, 3.52, 8.116, etc.

(b) 所以...為 becomes 所以...謂
燕民所以悅喜迎王師者, 謂齊救於水火之中耳 "The reason why the people of Yen received the King's armies with such pleasure was simply because Ch'i was saving them from "fire and flood" (i.e. from tyranny)" (2.16).

(c) 為 "do, become, create" becomes 謂
謂窮則獨善其身者也 "If you are impoverished, then cultivate your goodness in solitude" (2.25 (章)). 當謂何也 "What should I do?" (2.19). 謂此詩者 "he who composed this song" <u>Text</u> has 為此詩者 (2.87).

(d) 為 "delegation of agency" becomes 謂
有之於己乃謂人有之 "If you have it in yourself, then have it for others" (8.82).
(e) 謂 in the Text is read as though it were 為
Text: 此之謂 "describes this" but Commentary 是為不可活也 (2.88).

4.5. The Reflexive
i. The use of <u>Tzyh</u> in compounds

In Late Han as in LAC the reflexive is marked by the occurrence of <u>tzyh</u> 自 before the verb (see LAC 3.5.4.1). <u>Tzyh</u>, however, occurs in certain other forms of distribution, and is then often compounded with <u>gong</u> 躬, <u>shen</u> 身 "person, body" or <u>jii</u> 己 "self," etc. In the agential distributive position 躬自；躬；自身；身自 and 身 occur, when the agent is performing <u>in person</u>, usually where this is contrary to expectation. In the same position 獨身 occurs in the sense of "agent by himself, alone, to the exclusion of all others." Used with <u>jii</u> "self" <u>jii-tzyh</u> 己自 occurs as Agent. <u>Tzyh</u> also occurs in word-formation for reflexive action in such compounds as <u>tzyh-lih</u> 自利 "self-interest" (1.11); <u>tzyh-shiou</u> 自修 "self-cultivation" (1.93); 自由 "self-from" > "of own volition" (2.134.) <u>Tzyh-ran</u> 自然 "so-of-itself" > "natural," "spontaneous." (2.21, 7.76).

<u>Examples</u>
自 etc. in the agential distributive position
(a) "in person, personally, itself," 兵自殺之 "the weapon itself killed him" (1.31)
不用心於躬自耕也 "not put his mind to ploughing in person" (3.109.) 當身自具其食 "must prepare his food himself" (3.86)
必自身種粟乃食之邪 "must he personally have

grown his food, before he will eat?" (3.87), 自視何 "as you yourself see it, what ...? (3.14);
(b) "alone" 獨自作樂 "play music alone" (1.73).

ii. The use of the Emphatic and Reflexive Pronoun Jii

In both LAC and Late Han, the emphatic or reflexive pronoun is jii 己, "self," which occurs irrespective of person (referring to the speaker, the person addressed, and persons other than these), and is deployed indifferently in the agential and post-verbal positions. Jii also occurs as a determinative in syntagma, often marked with the particle of determination jy 之. Jii occurs with tzyh 自 in both jii-tzyh and tzyh-jii. Jii is used with much greater frequency in Late Han, and is often preferred in the Commentary where the Text has the non-reflexive pronouns.

Examples
(a) Jii, Jii-tzyh and Jii-shen in the agential position
己自狂曲何能正人 "When a man is himself crooked, how can he straighten others?" (4.8). 己所不欲勿施於人 "do not do to others those things you do not wish for yourself" (7.94 (章)). 非己身所能傳 "This is not something which one oneself can contrive" (2.29).
(b) Jii in the post-verbal position 識仁義之生於己也 "Realizing that Humanity and Justice are born within ourselves" (5.30). 非禮招己則不往 "if summoned by an improper Rite, he would not go" (4.2). 恐其污己也 "fearing that he would defile him" (2.107).

(c) <u>Jii</u> in syntagma

己之恥 "his own shame" (6.39) 己之賢才 "his own worth and capabilities" (2.108).

己親屬 "his own kith and kin" (3.120).

己之本性 "his own inate nature" (7.83).

己力 "one's own strength" (2.84).

自己之民 "their own people" (2.95 (章)).

自己作孽者 "those who bring retribution on themselves" (2.88).

(d) For <u>Jii</u> preferred to the non-reflexive pronoun, see section 2.1.i above, Note. On the Mician slogan "I act in my own interests" the <u>Commentary</u> observes 為我為己也 (8.6).

4.6　　　　　　AGENCY IN SUMMARY

LAC	LATE HAN	
	Changes in usage	Innovations in usage
吾；爾；etc.	>我；汝	
或；莫	> Obsolete	或 becomes selective conjunction
偕 "both"	>俱 "all" 俱 encroaches on 皆 俱；皆 > collective before verbs	
孰 "which?"	>誰 "who?"	
相	相, but also occurs parasitically	
交	> Obsolete, confused with 俱 謂 u.f. 爲	
爲	Confined to reflexive roles	
自		
己	Used with greater frequency	自己 etc.

The principal changes in the Agential Complex are shifts away from specialized forms, and their obsolescence, blunted usage, or parasitic retention, towards the use of single, all-purpose forms. These changes, as with those in syntagma and the verbal complex (see sections 2.7 and 3.7 above), are characteristics of the Archaic-Han Shift.

CHAPTER 5

CLAUSES, PHRASES AND ENDINGS
IN THE VERBAL SENTENCE

The principal changes in Late Han from LAC usage are: (i) the diminution of the role of *erl* for subordination, the re-introduction of the EAC form *jih* for subordination, and a tendency to replace the *erl* clause of LAC, with a greater complexity of clause assembly, and a greater variety of conjunctive devices (see 5.1); (ii) the parasitic occurrence of *erl* in the instrumental clause (see 5.2); (iii) greater complexity in clause assembly, leading to the redundance of the use of the anaphoric pronouns, with a consequent loss in both role and meaning for the anaphoric pronouns, both singly and in combinations (see 5.3); (iv) blunting in the use of the final particles, and a tendency to reduce the variety of final particles of LAC (see 5.4); (v) a new form of interrogative sentence (see 5.4.iii); (vi) changes in time and place indications (see 5.5).

5.1. The *Erl* Clause
    i. Diminution in the role of *Erl*
    The *erl* clause, interposed between the agent and the main verb, is of such common occurrence in LAC as to make *erl* 而 one of its particles of highest frequency, and the use of the *erl* clause a typical characteristic of LAC (see *LAC* 3.7). In Late Han, by contrast, the role of *erl* is almost exclusively conjunctive, usually adversative in some sense, "yet, but" and the like, with the consequence that *erl* clauses in the *Text* are very frequently rephrased in the *Commentary*. In such cases, Jaw Chyi either disregards *erl* altogether, or abstracts the subordinate

clause and restates it as a separate and coordinate clause. <u>Erl</u> is then replaced by a wide variety of conjunctions, <u>yii</u> 以; <u>ru</u> 如; <u>tzer</u> 則; <u>shyh-yih</u> 是亦, etc.

Clearly, by Late Han times <u>erl</u> has lost much of the precision of role and meaning it enjoys in LAC, and the <u>erl</u> clause has been largely replaced by a greater complexity of sentence structure. This greater complexity affects not only the role of <u>erl</u> but also that of the anaphoric pronouns, for which, see section 5.3 below.

<u>Examples</u>
(a) <u>Erl</u> disregarded
<u>Text</u> 王往而征之 "If having once set out, the King were to punish them ..." becomes 願王往征之也 "wished the King to set out and punish them" (1.38); <u>Text</u> 刺人而殺之 "Having stabbed a man, to kill him" becomes 用兵殺人 "to kill a man with a weapon" (1.31); <u>Text</u> 效死而民弗去 "If being faced with death, the people do not leave [the city]" becomes 至死使民不畔去 "If, when death approaches, this would not cause the people to leave [the city] in rebellion" (2.22). Other examples will be found in 5.7, 1.94, 2.128 etc.

(b) <u>Erl</u> avoided, by breaking into two clauses
<u>Text</u> 用之而成路 "being put to use, it becomes a road" becomes 用之不止則踐成為路 "if used continually, then the footpath is made into a road" (8.70); <u>Text</u> 四體不言而喻 "exemplified in every limb, without being expressed in words" becomes 口不言, 人以曉喻而知之 "Nothing is said with the mouth. But others, by the example manifested, know about it" (7.99) (for the use of <u>erl</u> here in the instrumental clause see section 5.2.i below); other examples will be found in 2.84, 1.37, 1.40, 3.25, 2.17 etc.

ii. The use of the Jih Clause

On the other hand, where Jaw Chyi resorts to a subordinate clause between agent and verb, he sometimes reverts to the EAC form, using jih 既 (for this see EAC 3.7).

Examples
Jih marks a subordinate clause
孟子既為齊宣王言之滕文公問 "Mencius, having explained this matter for Duke Hsüan of Ch'i, was asked by Duke Wen of T'eng ..." (3.57); 人既自有家復益韓魏百乘之家 "Men who, having estates of their own, further increase them with the hundred-chariot estates of Han and Wei ..." (7.85); 既不能得狂者欲得有介之人 "Being unable to get headstrong men, he wanted to get men of integrity ..." (8.114); 既不論三皇五帝殊無所問 "Not having discussed the Three Emperors and the Five Kings, there was absolutely nothing to inquire about" (1.48); 既去近留, "Having left, to stay so close" (3.31). See also 6.107, etc. For other Late Han usages of erl see section 3.2.v above and 7.1.ii below.

Note. The subordinate clause in jih is a further example of the resuscitation of EAC forms in Late Han. See section 3.4.v Note, above.

5.2. The Instrumental
i. Erl terminating the Instrumental Clause
In LAC, the erl clause (... 而) is verbal, and the instrumental phrase (以 ...) is substantival. (See LAC 3.6.1; 3.7.1.) In Late Han the instrumental clause occurs sporadically with a parasitic erl (以 ... 而).

Examples

人以曉喻而知之 "Others, by the example manifested, know about it" (7.99); 故以相配而言之也 "Therefore, by virtue of their respective suitability, they are mentioned" (8.122); 不以性欲而苟求之也 "does not, by following his natural inclinations, seek improperly for them" (8.78); 以己力不足而往服從於人 "to go and submit to others because one's own strength is insufficient [i.e., to resist]" (2.84). 以子噲不以天子之命而擅以國與子之 "thinking that, Tzu-k'uai had irresponsibly handed over the state to Tzu-chih, not having done so with a charge from the Son of Heaven" (3.8).

Note. For 謂 replacing 以為 see section 4.4.i above.

5.3. Anaphora

i. The use of Anaphora

In the evolution from LAC to Late Han, the anaphoric pronouns (pronouns used for repetition and recapitulation), chyi 其 and jy 之, become blunted and shift in meaning (for which, see sections 2.1.i, 2.3.i-iv above). This also happens to the allegro forms in which jy is incorporated (see paragraph ii below). But a more far-reaching change takes place, of which the blunting and shift of pronouns is but a symptom. This change is best illustrated with an example. In 3.48 the following passage occurs, which is here set out in a way so as to show the order of its phrase and clause assembly, by marking them from a to g; and to indicate the use of anaphora in making connections of phrases, by underlining the anaphoric pronouns.

諸侯之禮	a	The Rites for a Feudal Lord.
吾未之學也	b	I have not studied <u>them</u>.
雖然	c	Though <u>this</u> is so.
吾嘗聞之矣	d	I have learned <u>this</u> (i.e. the following.)
三年之喪 齊疏之服 飦粥之食	e	{Three years of mourning, the wearing of mourning clothes, the eating of plain food,
自天子達於庶人	f	from the Son of Heaven down to commoners,
三代共之	g	in the Three Dynasties, all practised <u>these</u>.

This passage is rendered in Late Han as follows, the rearrangement of clause and phrase being indicated by the use of the letters <u>a</u> to <u>g</u> (as above) within parenthesis.

我雖不學諸
侯之禮,嘗聞
師言三代以
前君臣皆行
三年之喪齊
疏齋食也

Though I have not studied the Rites for a Feudal Lord (<u>c</u> <u>b</u> <u>a</u>), I have heard my Master say (<u>d</u>) that, during and prior to the Three Dynasties, both Prince and Subject (<u>g</u> <u>f</u>) observed the three years' mourning period, mourning dress, and fasting (<u>e</u>).

Here, the rearrangement precludes the necessity for the use of recapitulatory pronouns.

In LAC, the anaphoric pronouns occur frequently and are used with precision and predictability. Their use is necessitated by the order of clause and phrase assembly. In Late Han a more supple order of assembly of phrase and clause reduces the necessity for the pronouns, and results in an eroding of the distinctions made by the pronouns which, in LAC, are strictly observed.

<u>Note</u>. It might be thought that the difference between <u>Mencius</u> and its paraphrase, illustrated above, is merely

one of style. Mencius achieves an *effect* by the use of disjointed phrases - a sort of range of emphases - while Jaw Chyi achieves an *effect* of smooth transition by his re-shuffling of the clause assembly. But if this is merely stylistic change, it is of the nature of permanent change, for it influences changes in the particles themselves. And it is not only the anaphoric pronouns that suffer blunting and loss of role. The entire repertory of grammatical particles display similar symptoms. Taken together, this suggests a fundamental change in the nature of the language which cannot be attributed merely to stylistic variation. In their totality, these features add up to the Archaic-Han shift - a shift of the grammatical burden borne by the "empty words" in LAC, to the "full words" in Late Han.[1]

ii. The eroding of the Anaphoric Pronouns
   in allegro forms

In LAC, the frequency of occurrence of the anaphoric pronouns results, where there is constant collocation with the post-verbal particle, in allegro forms. These are *yan* 焉 (於 + 之) and *ju* 諸 (之 + 於 or 之 + 乎). *Yan* and *ju* in the *Text* when rendered in the *Commentary* are constantly misunderstood, leading to minor misinterpretations of the *Text*. When used freely (particularly in the *Chapter Summaries*) *yan* and *ju* are either assimilated

---

[1] It might be added that when Jaw Chyi is writing in Classical style as in the *Chapter Summaries* he achieves the same effect of terse, disjointed phrases, but either fails to use the anaphoric pronouns or misuses them. This again suggests that the feature here described is not purely one of style. (See Appendix 2.)

with the final particles, or used simply for jy 之, or used parasitically, in a way that suggests that by Late Han they were no longer understood as allegro forms.

Examples

(a) 焉 in Text understood as "final particle" like 耳; 哉 etc.
Jaw Chyi defines 焉耳 in 1.20 as 焉耳者懇至之辭 "Yan eel are 'words' indicating emphatic finality." The passage reads 盡心焉耳 "I exert my mind in it [i.e. in governing my state] nothing more, nothing less." Here yan is 於之 "in it," but Jaw Chyi reads yan as being of a class with the final particle eel 耳. This understanding of yan colours the interpretation of many passages. 既竭心思焉 "having exhausted the thoughts of the mind in it" becomes 盡心欲行恩 "exhausting the mind, wishing to behave with kindness" (4.74); 不藏怒焉 "does not harbour resentment against him" becomes 不問善惡親愛之而已 "regardless of his behaving well or ill, loves him -- nothing less" (5.93); 何加焉 "what does that add to me," becomes 何加益哉 "what increase is there?" (6.113); 我不憾焉 "I am not vexed with him"(lit. "by him") becomes 無恨心耳 "had no hatred in his heart" (8.115).

(b) 焉 in Commentary used like 也 etc. or used parasitically. 其道一焉 "The Way is one!" (4.83 (章)); 恥之甚焉 "This is the extreme of disgrace" (5.70 (章)); Text 則必取盈焉 "then must collect full payment from them" becomes ... 必滿其常數焉 "They must pay in full the average [assessment]" (3.62); Text 何畏焉 "why be afraid of them" becomes 何畏齊楚焉 "why be afraid of Ch'i and Ch'u?" (4.31.) In the last two examples the yan in the Text is meaningful, but as used in the Commentary it is tautologous -- and thus parasitical.

(c) Misinterpretations arising from giving a wrong interpretation to yan in the Text. Text: 將為君子焉 "there will be gentlemen in that place." The Commentary first observes 為有也 "wei is yeou" and continues 有君子 "It has gentlemen" (3.73); Text: 毗焉 "made dull by it," is understood as 毗然 and defined as an attribute, 毗者蒙蒙目不明之貌 "the word mau means 'as though blindfold, the eye not seeing'"(4.108); Text: 納其貢稅焉 "took away his revenues from him" becomes 納其貢賦與之 "collected his revenues, and presented them to him" (5.93); Text: 日月有明容光必照焉 "If the sun or the moon is shining, their form and light are always reflected in them" becomes 大明照幽微 "the great lights [i.e. the sun and moon] shed light on the dark and obscure" (8.5).

(d) 焉 is read as, or used as 於. 君子知舜告焉不得而娶 "The True Gentleman knows that if Shun had informed them, he would not have been able to marry" (4.124.) Text: 君無尤焉 "The prince should not impute error to them" becomes 君無過責之 "The prince should not scold them for their faults" (2.20). Other examples of 焉 disregarded or misunderstood will be found in 5.40, 5.61, 6.118, 6.104, 7.83, 7.76, 7.98, 8.51, 8.54, 1.40, 1.31, 2.124, 3.24, 3.85, 3.108, 2.107.

(e) The use of ju

Ju 諸 is replaced by jy 之 in 3.92, 1.79, 3.11.
Ju 諸 is used for jy 之 in 5.39.
Ju 諸 is replaced by yu 於 in 1.58.
Ju 諸 is replaced by foou 否; jy-ye 之邪; jy-foou 之否; jy-foou hu 之否乎; bu 不; or jy-hu 之乎 in 5.105, 4.32, 5.116, 5.110, 1.72, 1.104, 2.7, 3.16.

5.4. The Final Particles
i. The loss of precision

The particles that occur at the end of sentences, and indicate the mood of the speaker, or impose an accentual pattern in LAC, are rendered with an abandon in the process of translation into Late Han that can only be described as chaotic. In LAC such particles are used with precision and predictability. In Late Han they lose this precision. If a statistical trend is of significance, Late Han seems to prefer ye 邪 for marking the interrogative; eel 耳 for marking heightened emotion (much more broadly than the 耳 = 而已 of LAC); and uses a new form of interrogative, final 不 and 否, for the alternative-choice sort of question.

Where final particles occur in allegro forms in LAC, (爾 for 而已; 諸 for 之乎; 與 for 也乎; 夫 for 否乎 etc.) they are either misunderstood in Late Han or used interchangeably with single particles. Jaw Chyi, for example, defines 爾 as 爾者歎而不怨之辭也 "The word eel is an interjection, but has no suggestion of resentment" (8.123), and 夫 as 歎辭 "a sigh-word," i.e. an interjection (6.64).

Thus the final particles, in common with many particles already described, display the same trend towards the erosion of meaning, the blunting of distinctions, and the reduction in role, that characterizes the Archaic-Han Shift.

Examples

Loss of precision in the use of the final particles. Hu 乎 is replaced by 也 as in 7.45, 6.46, 8.24; or by 否 as in 4.13, 5.128, 3.21; or by 邪 as in 3.87, 6.27, 7.24, 7.45, 3.37; or by 不邪 as in 4.111; or by 也乎 as in 8.123; and is supplied gratuitously in 3.24.

Hu is used for 哉 in 4.61; and for 與 in 6.28, 6.69.

THE VERBAL SENTENCE   65

Yu 與 by contrast is replaced by 矣 in 5.88; by 邪 in
6.68, 7.22, 6.81, 6.75, 6.64, 8.22, 8.91, 3.91, 4.59,
1.73, 6.68; by 也 in 4.59, 8.24, 6.68, 2.130; and
used wrongly in 8.91; disregarded in 3.16, 2.5; replaced by 乎 in 2.123, 3.12; and replaced by 否 in
3.12.
Tzai 哉 is replaced by 乎 in 4.61, 3.12, 3.37; or by 也
in 6.26; or by 邪 in 6.103. Yee 也 and yih 矣 inter-
change in 3.82, 2.73, 5.8, 8.112 (twice) 8.2, 8.70,
1.28, 3.35.
Yee in Text is disregarded in 6.34.
Yih in Text is disregarded in 3.43.
Yee is supplied gratuitously in 6.76, 3.91, 6.41,
3.20, 3.21.
Yih is supplied gratuitously in 3.12.
Yee is replaced by eel 耳 6.111, 6.120, 5.38, 3.37.
Yee replaces 爾 in 5.25.
Yee is replaced by 邪 in 1.34; by 乎 in 3.22.
Erl-yii-yih 而已矣 in Text is replaced by 也 in 8.89,
8.83, and by eel 耳 in 8.21 and in 7.93.

ii. The use of Foou and Ran
   In LAC ran 然 "it is so, yes!" and foou 否 "it is not
so, no!" standing alone, are answers of consent or dis-
sent to questions. Neither foou nor ran occur in this
usage in Late Han. The paraphrist defines foou as 不是
in 5.117 (following Yuann Yuan's 阮元 emendation, see
Jiau Shyun 正義 in loc.), and elsewhere almost invariably
replaces foou with a material answer and paraphrases ran.

   Examples
   (a) Foou as a simple "no" in answer to a question is
replaced by a material answer, or is explained 孟子
言否云舜不詐喜   "When Mencius says 'foou' he

is saying that Shun did not feign his pleasure" (5.88); Text 否 Commentary 言不然也 "it means not so" (5.97); Text 否 Commentary 堯不與之 "Yao did not give it"(5.105); Text 曰否 Commentary 曰不自織布 "he said he did not weave the cloth himself" (3.87); Text 否 Commentary 彭更曰不以舜為泰也 "P'eng Keng said 'I do not think Shun was gross'" (4.20); and Text 曰否 Commentary 彭更曰不然也 "P'eng Keng said, 'It was not so'" (4.23).

(b) Ran as a simple "yes" in answer to a question is replaced with a material answer. 以鐵耕乎曰然 "Does he plough with a ploughshare?" He answered 'yes'." The answer here in the paraphrase is 相曰用之 "Hsiang said 'He uses one'." (3.90); 然 "yes" becomes 如是 "as you say" in 3.53, 3.22, 3.16; see also 7.6.

iii. Foou and Bu as final interrogatives

Foou 否 and Bu 不 (bu as an innovation) in Late Han, however, occur at the end of sentences rendering them interrogative, in an alternative-choice form of questioning.

Examples
(a) Foou 不知可使寡人得相見否 "I do not know if you can arrange for us to see each other or not?" (2.117); 問君子之道當仕否 "He asked, 'According to the way of the True Gentleman, is it obligatory to give office [to a gentleman], or not?'" (4.13); 知肯就之否 "[so that I may] know is he willing to come or not?" (3.22); 不知誠有之否 "I do not know if this is in fact so or not?" (1.51). See also 3.90 and 3.21.
(b) Bu 足以笑百步止者不 "Are they in an adequate position to mock those who stopped after

THE VERBAL SENTENCE   67

running a hundred paces?" (1.22); 王有是語不 "Did your Majesty say this or not?" (1.72). See also 2.76, 6.113.

Note. The final interrogative bu in the above examples is in certain editions replaced by foou 否. But final 不 can be attested as Han usage in other authors, for example in Hann Shu. See, for example, 楊樹達詞詮 s.v. 不 p. 18 paragraph 5.

5.5. Time and Place
   i. Shyi becomes obsolescent
The common indication of past time in LAC is shyi 昔 or shyi-jee 昔者, which may indicate "yesterday," "a few days ago," or "in far antiquity" (see LAC 3.10). Wherever shyi is paraphrased it is replaced consistently. For "yesterday" it is replaced by tzwo-ryh 昨日 (a Late Han innovation), for "a few days ago" by woang 往 (昔者往也，謂數日之間也 shyi is woang and means "after an interval of several days") (4.121) and for the far past by woang-jee 往者. This is so consistent, that shyi evidently was obsolescent in Late Han.

   Examples
   Shyi-jee or shyi is replaced by tzwo-ryh in 2.118 and 2.119, by woang-ryh in 2.4, and by woang-jee in 1.107, 1.94, 2.74, 3.29 and 5.64. See also 3.22.

   Note. Wang Yih in his Commentary on the Li Sau also explains shyi as woang. See Jiau Shyun's Jenq-yih 1.94.

   ii. Miscellaneous
   Ta-ryh 他日 "a day other than the day in question" is defined as yih-ryh 異日 in 4.61 and yih-ryh replaces ta-ryh in 4.62.
   Shyy 始 is used equally in LAC and Late Han in the time position for "prior to this" and in the aspectual

position for "for the first time." 始作俑者 is, however, rendered 本由有作俑者 (1.33) yielding been-you "for first time" as an innovation in Late Han.

Wei-jian 為間 for "after a short time, after an interval" in both its occurrences in Mencius elicits comment from Jaw Chyi. In 3.124 he defines it as 有頃之間也 and in 8.70 為間有間也; Jiau Shyun in his Jeng-yih (3.125) observes that Gau Yow defines 有間 in Leu-shyh Chuen-Chiou as 頃, and 間 in Jann-gwo Tseh as 須臾 and 有間 in Lieh Tzyy is defined as 小時也, which suggests that 頃 and 須臾 had replaced wey jian by Late Han times.

Yu tzwu 於卒 and tzwu 卒 occur in LAC as "finally, in the end." In 8.76 Jaw Chyi defines this as 卒後也 and in 6.43 as 於卒末後復來時也. Jaw Chyi, however, uses tzwu himself in 6.25 卒與之天位 "Finally, he presented him with the Throne of Heaven." In 5.42 竟如孺子之所言 "In the end, it transpired just as Ju Tzu had said," jing 竟 performs this function.

5.6   CLAUSES, PHRASES AND ENDINGS IN THE VERBAL SENTENCE IN SUMMARY

LAC	LATE HAN	
	Changes in usage	Innovations in usage
Erl clause (以...) 焉 諸 與 夫 也 矣 昔	avoided 既 for subordination (以...而) Assimilated into final particles, use blunted, or becomes parasitic Distinction blunted > 往	不 否 as final interrogatives 本 由 "for first time" 昨日 "yesterday"

    The verbal sentence of LAC, with its simple structure, its *erl* and instrumental clauses neatly demarked, and its prolific use of resuming pronouns to indicate the interrelationships of sentences, is thus replaced with a looser, more complex clause and sentence structure. In this process, the anaphoric pronouns and *erl* suffer diminution in role, semantic change, and blunting of usage. This reduction in role is characteristic of the Archaic-Han shift as has already been noted (see sections 2.7, 3.9, 4.6, above). But it is also a characteristic of the Archaic-Han shift that sentences are greatly expanded and their interrelationships are more complex. These relationships are marked, not by resuming pronouns and demonstratives, but by conjunctions. The greater expansiveness of the sentence lessens the role that the final particles of LAC play.

CHAPTER 6

THE DETERMINATIVE SENTENCE

In the Determinative Sentence the principal changes in Late Han from LAC usage are: (i) the establishment of shyh as a copula in free or non-contrastive usage, the introduction of dann as a copula, and the compounding of the copulae of common inclusion; (ii) the introduction of yuan as a causal particle.

6.1. The Copulae

    i. Shyh as a Copula

Shyh 是 occurs as a copula in LAC, only as a contrastive form for fei 非 (see LAC 4.4.1). In Late Han shyh occurs freely as a copula in the determinative sentence.

Examples

柳下是其號也 "Liu-hsia is his courtesy name" (2.108); 豈非皆是人之子乎 "[Both commoners and princes alike], surely it cannot but be, all are somebody's son!" (8.24); 今此時亦是其一時也 "Today, the present period is, too, one of these periods" (3.35); 人所謂是舊國也 "What men say is an ancient state ... " (2.3).

Note. Shyh also occurs freely in Late Han both as a determinative demonstrative 是仁道 "this Humane Way" (2.103), 是詩 "this poem" (1.55); and as a pregnant demonstrative 無大於是者也 "There is nothing greater than this" (2.121).

ii. **Dann** as a copula

In Late Han, dann 但 occurs between the two terms of a determinative sentence in the sense of A is merely B, and also (like fei 非 and shyh 是 in LAC) as the Determined Term, in the sense of "It is merely ...." In this sense both dann 但 and dann wei 但為 occur. The negated form of dann in this usage is fei dann 非但.

Examples
(a) <u>Dann</u> as copula. 此亦但志食也 "This, after all, is merely a matter of being concerned about food" (4.22); 羽旆之美，但飾羽旄使之美好也 "The splendour of the feathered plumes is merely the splendour of feather decorations" (1.77).
(b) <u>Dann</u> as Determined Term. 但義盡耳 "It is merely a just thing pressed too far" (6.31); 但不以無為有耳 "It is merely a matter of not taking the lack for the possession" (2.82).
(c) <u>Dann-wei</u> as Determined Term. 但為合眾之行 "In fact, this is merely conforming with the crowd" (8.115). See also 1.99, 2.80.
(d) <u>Dann</u> negated with <u>fei</u>. 非但與姜女俱行而已也 "It was not merely that he and the Lady Chiang travelled together" (1.113). 人所謂是舊國也非但見其有高大樹木也 "What men describe as being an ancient state, is not merely one in which tall trees can be seen" (2.3). (When dann is negated with bu it is determining a verb, as, for example, in 不但坐而聽命 "He does not merely sit, awaiting the dictates of fate" (8.79). Thus 不但 and 非但 contrast.)

iii. **Jyi** as a copula
Late Han uses jyi 即 as a copula, as does LAC, but jyi before verbs in Late Han is aspectual (see 3.2.vi).

THE DETERMINATIVE SENTENCE

Examples

萬子即萬章也 "Wan Tzu is, in fact, Wan Chang" (8.116); 離朱即離婁也 "Li Chu is, in fact, Li Lou (4.64). 此即人之疢疾也 "This is, in fact, the sickness of mankind" (7.95).

iv. Compounding of Copulae of Common Inclusion

The copulae of common inclusion (A is like B) of LAC ru 如 ruoh 若 and you 猶 (but not you 由 which is obsolescent in this usage in Late Han (see section 3.5.ii above) occur unchanged in Late Han. When introducing a simile, however, they tend to combine with pih 譬, thus pih-ru 譬如; pih-ruoh 譬若; and pih-you 譬猶

Examples
(a) Pih-ru. Text has ru but Commentary has pih-ru in 8.84. See also 3.12, 8.108.
(b) Pih-ruoh. See 8.73, 7.93, 2.88, 3.116 (章).
(c) Pih-you. Text has you but Commentary has pih-you in 4.87, 2.85.

6.2. Cause and Consequence

i. The use of Yuan

In 因 introduces a clause of cause in both LAC and Late Han, in the sense of "because." Late Han also has yuan 緣 with the same function and meaning.

Examples

後世緣此遂征商人 "In later generations, because of this, merchants were accordingly taxed" (3.25); 聖人緣人心而制禮也 "The Sages, because of human feelings, instituted [burial] rites" (3.123) which is similar to 聖人緣情制禮奉終 "The Sages because of human emotions, instituted rites for the service of the dead" (3.125 (章)). See 2.82; 5.9.

Note. Guh 故 "cause" occurs before verbs in the sense of "for good cause," "deliberately," "with something in mind." Yuan is also used in this sense. 孟子雖心知王意而故問者欲令王自道，遂緣以陳之 "Though Mencius knew in his heart what was in the King's thoughts, he deliberately asked this question, because he wanted to make the King say so himself. Accordingly, with this in mind, he posed the question" (1.61). See also section 2.5.i above, for the use of jee 者 in marking causal clauses.

6.3   THE DETERMINATIVE SENTENCE
                    IN SUMMARY

LAC	LATE HAN	
	Changes in usage	Innovations in usage
是 (in contrast to 非)	是 in free usage	但；非但 譬如；譬若； 譬猶. 緣 (causal)
如；若；猶 >		
由 >	Obsolescent	

   As with the verbal sentence (see section 5.6 above), the Archaic Han Shift is marked in the Determinative Sentence with a greater use of the connectives, which, as with the conjunctions of the verbal sentence, come into greater play as the clause structure becomes more complex.

CHAPTER 7
CONJUNCTIONS

The principal changes in Late Han from LAC usage among the conjunctions are: (i) The encroachment of fuh 復 upon the role of yow 又 (see 7.1.i) and the development of adversative conjunctions (see 7.1.ii and iii). (ii) The marking of both the protasis and the apodosis in Conditional Clauses (see 7.2.i), the obsolescence of goou 苟, shinn 信 (see 7.2.ii) and sy 斯 (see 7.2.iii), and the introduction of jiow 就 (see 7.2.v). (iii) The introduction of new forms of concession, tzyh 自 for conditioned concession (see 7.3.i), taang 儻 for required concession (see 7.3.ii), and shanq 尚 in a new form of concession (see 7.3.iii).

7.1. Co-ordinate sequence

The conjunctions yow 又 "too, also" and yih 亦 "also, after all" of LAC (see LAC 5.1) continue in use into Late Han. The role of yow 又, however, is encroached upon by fuh 復 which, in this usage, is an innovation in Late Han. Chiee 且 "moreover" also occurs as a conjunction, but in its aspectual role shifts from potential to momentary aspect (see section 3.2.i above).

i. Fuh as a Co-ordinate Conjunction

Yow 又 "and too, also, as well" in the Text is replaced by fuh 復 in the Commentary in 2.17, and by you-fuh 又復 in 8.84. It occurs singly, and in the compounds tzer-fuh 則復 "and, furthermore," bwu-fuh 不復 "but did not also," and yow-fuh 又復 "but in addition."

Examples

出疆何為復載質 "When travelling beyond the state frontier, why did he also carry a gift?" (4.18); 今復并燕一倍之地 "but now, in addition, you have incorporated territory from Yen ..." (Text has 今又) (2.17); 追而還之,入蘭則可,又復從而宵之 "having chased [the stray pig] and returned it, and put it into its sty, that will do. But to go on and hobble it as well ... (8.84); 但加載書,不復歃血 "they merely attached the document [to the sacrifice], but did not perform the blood-smearing ceremony as well" (7.37); 父兄百官且復言也 "His elders and officials, furthermore, said"-- Text has 且曰 ("furthermore said") (3.51); 彼不復問孰可,使自往伐之 "They did not also ask me 'who should [attack Yen],' but, of their own volition, immediately went off and attacked it" (3.12). See also 8.42, 3.106; etc.

ii. The Adversative

In section 5.1.i above, <u>erl</u> 而 is described as having lost much of its LAC role and meaning in Late Han, and to have shifted to use as a conjunction. In section 3.2.v one of those conjunctive functions is illustrated. This is to supply the adversative, for clauses following a <u>dann</u> clause (for example, 但食之而不愛 "merely to feed him, but not to love him" (8.27)). But <u>erl</u> is not confined to the adversative and occurs for simple connection "and" and for mild concession "yet."

In section 3.2.v <u>Note</u> above, two examples are cited, which suggest that <u>dann</u> 但 by Late Han times is moving towards its later use as an adversative conjunction.

CONJUNCTIONS

Examples

(a) <u>Erl</u> as an adversative. 孔子以舜年五十而思慕其親不怠稱曰孝之至矣 "Because Shun was fifty years old, but still thought with sorrow of his parents' neglect of him, Confucius called him 'the filial son <u>par excellence</u>'" (7.15); 其人自以所行為是而無仁義之實 "This sort of person thinks his own course of conduct right, but lacks the reality of Humanity and Justice" (8.117); 其富貴已美矣而其人欿然不以足 "His wealth and honours would already be of great splendour, but such a man is indifferent and does not think this enough" (7.85).

(b) <u>Erl</u> for simple connection. 其事遠而難 "These matters are remote, and difficult" (4.98); 則通而易 "then it is close at hand and easy of access" (4.98 (章)).

(c) <u>Erl</u> for mild concession. 其好戰殘民與鄰國同而猶望民之多 "He loved warfare and oppressed his people, in just the same way as his neighbouring rulers did, yet he still hoped for his population to increase" (1.23). 季孫知孟子意不欲而心欲使孟子就之 "Chi-sun knew that Mencius at heart did not want to, yet still in his own mind he wanted to make Mencius go [and accept]" (3.23).

iii. The use of <u>Faan</u> "on the contrary"
Late Han uses <u>faan</u> 反 "turn over, come back,"[1] in a

---

[1] <u>Faan</u> 反 in <u>Mencius</u> is used in the sense of "turn over," literally, in the sense of "turning over the hand" (e.g. in 2.39), figuratively, in sense of "turning over in the mind -- reflecting upon" (e.g. in 2.55) and in <u>faan fuh</u> 反覆 "over and over" repeatedly (e.g.

conjunctive usage, "to the contrary," which implies a very strong adversative. This usage does not occur in LAC.

Examples

若欲急長苗而反使之枯死也 "It is like wanting to hasten the growth of plants, but, on the contrary, to cause them to wither to death" (2.66); 非徒無益於苗而反害之 "It is not merely of no benefit to the plants, on the contrary, it harms them" (2.68) (Text here has the conjunction yow 又 "but also"); 我欲行禮故不歷位而言反以我為簡易也 "I wished to observe the Rites, and so did not break ranks to speak [to him], but [he], to

in 6.59.) Faan is used in the sense of "turn round," hence "to come back to" "to revert to" (e.g. in 3.43 and 8.119) and causatively "make come back" — — "return property to" (2.18). In an extended sense it is used for "return to, repay, requite" (e.g. in 2.51). It is used in the sense of "turn against" hence "to contravene" (e.g. in 3.49) and in faan donq 反動 "a reaction" (see for example 2.59). In Late Han faan also occurs, but for the series "come back to" "return to" etc. Late Han prefers hwan 還 (5.64, 2.18, 3.32, 3.43, 8.24, 8.84, etc.).

In other senses, baw 報 "to requite" (e.g. in 2.51) and guei 歸 "to revert to" (e.g. in 8.119) substitute for faan. Faan as a conjunction is, however, an innovation in Late Han.

This study is restricted to a comparison of the grammatical features in Text and Commentary. The Commentary, however, offers — — as the above example shows — — an excellent source for a historical study of the development of the lexicon from Late Archaic to Han.

the contrary, thinks I behaved with laxity!" (5.53); 今之為關反以征稅 "Frontiers today, on the contrary, are used to impose taxes" (8.57); see also 4.22, 3.92, 4.89, 8.95 etc.

7.2. Conditioned Sequence
    (a) Marking the Protasis
    i. Ru-shyy, ru, jea-shyy and shyy

In conditioned sequences in LAC it is the apodosis that is marked by conditional conjunctions. (See LAC 5.3.) The protasis has the verb modally determined by ru 如 ruoh 若 etc. But already in LAC (for example in Moh Tzyy) these modal determinants with shyy 使 form a true conjunction ruoh-shyy 若使, and then precede the agent of the protasis.

In Late Han, the conditional conjunctions marking the protasis regularly precede the agent. They occur in the forms ru-shyy 如使, ru 如, jea-shyy 假使 and shyy 使. Shyy 使 in this usage is an innovation in Late Han.

    Examples
Ru-shyy, jea-shyy, ru and shyy: 如使夷子葬其父母也厚是以所賤之道奉其親也如其薄也 "If Yi Tzu buried his parents with extravagant rites, then he was rendering service to his own kin in a way he himself despises, but if he did so with inexpensive rites ..." (3.119); 如使在王左右者皆非居州之疇王當誰與為善乎 "If, among the King's courtiers, no one is a man of the order of [Hsüeh] Chü-chou, with whom can the King associate in doing good?" (4.33); 如使賢者棄愚不養其所當養則賢亦近愚矣 "If those who are competent abandon the inept, not looking after those whom they should look after, then the competent themselves

are not far removed from the inept" (5.15); 使我得志不居此堂也 "Even if I had my way, I would not live in such houses" (8.101); 假使如子濯孺子之得尹公之他而教之何由有逢蒙之禍 "Suppose now [that P'eng Meng had been taught by Yi Yin] just as Tzu-cho Ju-tzu had been taught by Yin-kung Chih-t'a how could the calamity of a P'eng Meng have happened?" (5.42). See also 3.115, 6.120, 2.4, 2.116, 2.48, 2.73, 2.62, 2.80, etc.

ii. Cherng replaces Goou

In LAC, goou 苟, shinn 信 and cherng 誠, introducing the protasis of a conditional statement, occur in the sense of "If indeed, if in fact" etc. (see LAC 5.3.2). Both goou and shinn in this usage are obsolescent in Late Han. Goou is defined in 1.11 and 5.26 苟誠也 and is consistently replaced by cherng, in the Commentary. In one instance the replacement is inappropriate, for the Text uses goou 苟 "improperly" in 不欲為苟去 "he did not want, for an improper reason, to leave" which is rendered 誠欲急去 "he really did want to leave quickly" (7.30). LAC used shinn before verbs in a modal sense, as an emphatic indicative. This, too, is replaced in Late Han by cherng.

Examples
(a) Cherng replaces goou in 1.67, 2.24, 2.99 (twice); 4.31, 5.26, 5.48, 6.105 (twice); 7.56 (twice); 8.59, 8.91.
(b) Cherng replaces shinn in 2.94 and replaces modal shinn in 水誠無分於東西 "Water indeed does not differentiate between east and west, but ..." (6.66).

CONJUNCTIONS

(b) Marking the Apodosis

iii. **Tzer** 則 replaces **Sy** 斯

The protasis is typically marked in LAC by tzer 則 but, in Mencius, also by sy 斯. Sy is obsolescent in Late Han, and is replaced by tzer 則.

Examples
Tzer replaces sy in 2.21, 1.31, 4.35, 5.9.
Tzer-sy replaces sy in 8.91 and occurs in 1.32 (章)
Sy-tzer replaces sy in 8.112.
Ruoh-tzer replaces sy in 6.27.

iv. **Tzer** replaced by **Tsyy** or **Dang**

Tzer 則 itself is replaced occasionally in Late Han by tsyy 此 or dang 當.

Examples
Tzer is replaced by tsyy in 2.9.
Tzer is replaced by dang in 2.1, 2.2 (twice) and 2.19.

v. **Jiow** in Conditioned Sequences

Jiow 就 occurs in Late Han as a verb "to approach to" "to come to" etc. and in this usage jiow occurs as early as the Book of Songs. But in the two examples given below, jiow seems close to its role in Modern Chinese.

Examples
(a) Jiow-shyy 就使 and jiow 就 as ? ruoh-shyy 若使 and ? tzer 則 堯舜之世皆行仁義故好戰殃民者不能自容也就使慎子能使魯一戰取齊南陽之地且猶不可 "In their day Yao and Shun practised Humanity and Justice and so such things as love of warfare and oppression of the people they would not tolerate. If Shen Tzu can make Lu do

battle to recover the territory of Nanyang from Ch'i, then that would be even more intolerable" (7.42); 今之所謂君子,非真君子也.順過非就為之辭 "The so-called princes of today are not true Princes. When they pursue an erroneous course, or exhibit an impropriety, <u>then</u> they make excuses for it" (3.18).

(b) Occurrences of <u>jiow</u> in verbal senses. <u>Jiow</u> occurs as verb in 來就為卿 "when you came, you became a minister" (3.20); 知肯就之否 "so that I may know if he is willing to come or not?" (3.22); see also 4.3, 7.35, 4.8 (章).

7.3. Concession

The Concessive Conjunctions <u>swei</u> 雖 and <u>swei-ran</u> 雖然 continue in use without change in Late Han. But two important innovations are introduced for special kinds of concession.

i. The use of <u>Tzyh</u>

<u>Tzyh</u> 自 occurs as an innovation in Late Han[2] for conditioned concession, in the sense of "even if, even though" (see also section 3.5.i above).

<u>Examples</u>
此吾人者自有獻子之家富貴而復有德不肯與獻子友也 "These five men, even though they honoured the House of Hsien-Tzu as being rich and noble but virtuous too, were unwilling to put themselves on the level of friendship with Hsien-tzu"

---

[2] <u>Tzyh</u> 自 used for conditioned concession also occurs in other Han writers. Examples occurring in <u>Shyy-jih</u> (史記) and <u>Hann-shu</u> (漢書); for example, will be found in Yang Shuh-dar, <u>Tsyr Chyuan</u> p. 364 <u>s.v.</u> <u>tzyh</u>.

(6.21). 管仲自魯囚執於士官,桓公舉以為相國 "Kuan Chung, even though in Lu he was imprisoned by the Leader of the Knights, was promoted by Duke Huan to the position of Premier" (7.59).

ii. <u>Taang</u> as a concessive conjunction

The introduction of <u>taang</u> 儻 to indicate a required condition is also an innovation in Late Han. <u>Taang</u> introduces a clause in the sense of "assuming that, provided that, always supposing that" etc.

<u>Examples</u>
如一見之,儻得行道,可以輔致霸王乎 "If once he [Mencius] met with them [the Feudal Lords], provided that he was enabled to put his Way into effect, could he not as a result assist them to become Paramount Prince?" (4.1). 王欲見之,先朝,使人往謂孟子云寡人如就見者(言就孟子之館相見也)有惡寒之病,不可見風,儻可來朝欲力疾臨視朝,因得見孟子也 "The King wished to see him [Mencius], so before dawn he sent a messenger to go and say to Mencius 'I was going to see you' (i.e. he was going to Mencius' residence). But the King had a cold, and could not expose himself to the wind. Provided that [Mencius] could come to Court, he would force [himself, despite] his illness, graciously to see him there, and as a result, he would [still] be able to see Mencius" (2.117).

iii. The use of <u>Shanq</u> in Concession

<u>You</u> 猶 and <u>shanq</u> 尚 (and <u>you-shanq</u> 猶尚) occur in LAC in a form of concession, in the sense of "even so, nevertheless" etc. (see <u>LAC</u> 5.4.3). <u>You</u> in this sense is obsolescent in Late Han, its function being assimilated

into shanq. Shanq, however, occurs in a form of concession, in which an extreme case of something more generally implied is conceded, often set off against the general implication. Shanq, in such cases, occurs *after* the statement of the extreme case.

Examples

仁者尚不肯為況戰鬬教人以求廣土地乎 "Even for a Humane man he would be unwilling to do this, and how much less for one who murders people by engaging in wars seeking thereby to enlarge his territory?" (7.45); 陶器者寡,尚不可以為國,況無君子之道乎 "Even when potters are in short supply one cannot govern a state, how much less can one do so without the Way of the True Gentleman?" (7.51); 如是歌哭者尚能變俗 "Even such people as these, singers and mourners, can change customs!" (7.27); 虞人不得其招尚不往,如何君子而不待其招 "Even a huntsman, without the appropriate summons, would not go, so what would be said of a Gentleman who did not await the appropriate summons?" (4.2); 周公太公地尚不能滿百里 "Even the lands of the Duke of Chou and of the T'ai-kung could not exceed a hundred miles square" (7.45).

7.4 CONJUNCTIONS IN SUMMARY

LAC	LATE HAN	
	Changes in usage	Innovations in usage
又 而 (subordinate) >	又 復 而 (conjunctive)	反 (strongly adversative)
如 若 (modal) >	如 若 (conjunctive) 如使；假使	
苟 信 誠 >	obsolescent 誠	
斯 (conditional)	replaced by 則 此 當 conditional	就 (for condition)
	自 (concession)	僅 (concession)
猶 (concession) > 尚	尚 尚 ("even a")	

The conjunctions thus increase in variety, tend towards compounding, and enjoy far greater frequency of occurrence. This, as has already been noted in 5.6 and 6.3 above, is characteristic of the Archaic-Han Shift.

CHAPTER 8

S U B S T I T U T I O N

The principal changes in Late Han from LAC among the substitutes are: (i) The blunting of the distinction made in the pronouns and demonstratives between determinative and pregnant forms, and the consequent obsolescence of certain LAC forms and the weakening and blunting of others (see 8.1 and 8.2). (ii) The obsolescence of the interrogatives yan 焉 and u and u-hu 惡, 惡呼 and their replacement by an 安 (see 8.3.i); the obsolescence of shi 奚 and shwu 孰 and their replacement by her 何 and shwei 誰 (see 8.3.iii, iv); the occurrence of her in new compound forms (see 8.3.v). (iii) The introduction of two new interrogatives, ninq 寧 and tserng 曾 (see 8.3.ii, viii). (iv) Changes in the syntactical deployment of the interrogative substitutes (see 8.3.vi).

8.1. The Pronouns
   i. The Personal Pronouns
   Two shifts, as already noted (see sections 2.1.i, 4.1.i above), occur from LAC to Late Han, in the use of the personal pronouns. These are
(i) The tendency for the determinative forms wu and eel to become assimilated with the pregnant forms woo and ruu, and for the pregnant forms to assume indifferently the agential and post-verbal roles.
(ii) When the personal pronouns are possessive, to mark this with the particle of determination jy 之. This gives

	Pronoun	Possessive Adjective
First person	woo 我	woo-jy 我之
Second person	ruu 汝	*ruu-jy 汝之

with a possibility, as variants, of wu 吾 and wu-jy 吾之 and eel 爾 and eel-jy 爾之.

Note 1. In the Archaic-Han shift, therefore, the pronouns move perceptibly towards the woo/woo-de and nii/nii-de of Modern Standard Chinese.

Note 2. Among the status pronouns (for which Jaw Chyi gives accurate descriptions, see Appendix 4), LAC Goa-ren 寡人, used by princes when speaking of themselves, is consistently replaced by woo 我 (and, in one instance, by Chyi 齊 (i.e. "the King of Ch'i"); see 1.20, 1.110, 1.112, etc.

ii. The Anaphoric Pronouns

No shift, to parallel that of the personal pronouns, occurs in the anaphoric pronouns chyi 其 and jy 之 except that the differentiation between them is occasionally blurred (see section 2.2.i above). Chyi 其 assumes a new demonstrative role (see section 2.3.ii). The main shift, as already described in section 5.3.i, is in the greatly reduced role played by anaphora itself. Because of this, the pronoun jy 之, when incorporated into allegro forms, tends to become absorbed into the final particles (see section 5.3.ii above). This weakening leads, occasionally, to replacing jy in the Text by tsyy-wuh 此物 "this thing" or tsyy-ren 此人 "this person," tsyy-shyh 此事 "this happening" or, when jy is replacing a pronoun, by jii 己 "self," or woo 我 "me."

Examples
Text 尊者賜之曰其所取之者義乎不義乎
Commentary 孟子曰今尊者賜己己問其所取此物

"Mencius said that if an honourable man gives a gift to us and we ask from whom he obtained it ..." [lit. "this thing"] (6.27); Text 何以謂之狂也 Commentary 何以謂此人為狂也 "Why did he call them [lit. "these people"] headstrong?" (8.114); Text 士則茲不悅 Commentary 士於此事不悅也 "As far as I [i.e. Yin Shih] am concerned, this is displeasing (3.31); Text 無處而餽之是貨之也 Commentary 義無所處而餽之是以貨財取我 "To give a gift to me when no just occasion merits one is to procure me with a bribe" (2.128); Text 竊聞之 Commentary 竊聞師言 "I heard [this >] my teacher say" (2.75); Text 於傳有之 Commentary 於傳文有是言 "In the Records handed down, there is this" [i.e. these words) (1.80).

8.2. The Demonstratives

Mention, too, has already been made (section 2.3.i) of the blunting of the distinction made in LAC between determinative and pregnant forms of the demonstrative. Sy 斯 and jy 之, the determinative demonstratives of LAC, become obsolete, and tsyy 此 and shyh 是 play the major role. Chyi 其, on the other hand, acquires a demonstrative role (see section 2.3.ii above).

8.3. The Interrogative Substitutes

The system of interrogative substitution, which, in LAC, has forms restricted to and specialized in almost every element in the sentence, tends in Late Han towards the redundancy of specialized forms, and towards simplification, the substitute role converging on certain all-purpose interrogatives. Thus yan 焉 and u 惡 u-hu 惡呼 in the Time and Place position are assimilated into an 安; the distinction between shwu 孰 and shwei 誰 is blurred and the role of both is assumed by shwei. Shi 奚 her 曷 and hwu 胡 become obsolescent, and are replaced by the all-purpose her 何.

There is, too, parallel with similar developments already described elsewhere, a tendency towards the use of periphrasis (her 何, for example, is expanded according to need to her-deeng 何等, her-ren 何人, etc.) and a tendency for substitutes to occur after the verb, where, in LAC because of polarity, they occur before the verb, as for example when her-wey 何謂 becomes wey-her 謂何, shwei yeu 誰與 becomes yeu shwei 與誰, and forms like yun-her 云何 occur.

Late Han also has two new interrogatives ning 寧 and tserng 曾.

i. The assimilation by An of Yan and U and U-hu

In LAC yan 焉 occurs in the Time and Place position, and asks "when?" "what time for?" "where?" and "whither?" U 惡 and u-hu 惡呼 in the Place position substitute for the element that appears, in non-interrogative statements, in the second post-verbal position. They ask "where?" "whither?" but also "by whom?" or "by what?" where the verb is passive.

In Late Han both yan and u are obsolete, and are replaced by the all-purpose an 安.

Examples
(a) Yan is replaced by an in 8.52, 5.7, 4.103, 4.109, 2.128, 4.10.
(b) U and u-hu are replaced by an in 8.15, 4.126, 4.109, 6.38, 7.53, 1.88, 1.41, 3.22, 1.33, 3.63, 3.86, 3.117, 4.61, 3.32.
(c) An occurs in Commentary in 2.16, 6.51, 8.119, 8.98.

SUBSTITUTION 91

(d) <u>Her</u> substitutes for <u>yan</u> in 8.3, 2.103, 2.108.
(e) <u>Her</u> substitutes for <u>u</u> in 2.123.
(f) <u>Chii</u> substitutes for <u>u</u> in 8.22.

Note. U 惡 as an interjection is also obsolescent in Late Han. It is defined as a "deep sigh" in 2.121, "an interjection expressing unease" in 2.74, and is replaced by the verb <u>tann</u> 歎 "to sigh" in 3.14.

ii. The use of <u>Ninq</u>

An 安 occurs in the Time and Place position in Late Han as an interrogative substitute. <u>Ninq</u> 寧 (which shares certain affinities with <u>an</u>, for example both mean "peace, to pacify") occurs in Late Han as an interrogative substitute in the position occupied by such words as <u>kee</u> 可 <u>neng</u> 能, expressing ability, possibility, and the like. <u>Ninq</u> in such contexts asks "could?" "can?"

Note. <u>Ninq</u> occurs in the <u>Commentary</u> as a verb in 8.16 "bring peace to." In its other occurrences it is (i) interrogative and (ii) in the "agential state" position. It is tempting to regard <u>ninq</u> as an interrogative form of <u>neng</u> (*nieng, *nəng). None of the conventional dictionary definitions of <u>ninq</u> (as, for example, <u>Tsyr Hae</u> 願詞 "expressing wish or preference"; 何也 "how?"; <u>chii</u> 豈也 "surely not?") account adequately for Jaw Chyi's use of <u>ninq</u>.

Examples
<u>Text</u> 可得聞與 "could I hear about that?" becomes 寧可得聞邪 (1.73). <u>Text</u> 有諸 "was there such a thing?" becomes 寧有之 "could such a thing be?" (1.79). <u>Text</u> 雖欲耕得乎 "Even though he wanted to plough, could he have managed to?" becomes 寧得耕乎 "would he have been able to plough?" (3.97). <u>Text</u> 可復許乎 "could [you] promise to bring them

about once more?" becomes 寧可復興乎 "Could [you] once again revive?" (Jaw Chyi explains 許猶興也 hence his interpretation of this sentence) (2.35). Text 如此則動心否乎 "If this happened, would you be moved or not?" becomes 如是寧動心畏難 "If this happened, could you be moved, or have fear for difficulties?" (2.48). Other examples occur in 3.90, 1.106, 6.27, 7.4.

iii. The assimilation of Shwu by Shwei
The assimilation of the agential distributive interrogative shwu 孰 into the more general interrogative substitute shwei 誰 has already been described in section 4.2.iv above.

iv. The obsolescence of Shi 奚
Jaw Chyi defines shi 奚 in 5.87 as 奚何也 and consistently replaces shi in the Text by her. Where shi-wey 奚為 occurs in the Text it is replaced by her-wey 何為, but her-wey also occurs as a replacement for shi alone. Shi evidently is obsolescent in Late Han.

Examples
Her replaces shi in 3.89, 8.19, 6.33, 7.8, 7.4, 1.69, 8.73.
Her-wey replaces shi-wey in 3.89, 7.55, 2.15, 2.31.
Her-wey replaces shi in 5.55, 6.34, 5.87.

v. Expansions of LAC Her
Her 何 substitutes at all levels, syntagmatic, sentential, and intra-sentential in LAC (see LAC 6.5). In Late Han certain of these levels are differentiated by periphrasis.
Where, in LAC, her occurs before a noun, in sense of "what sort of" "what kind of," Late Han has her-deeng 何

等 ; where her occurs in LAC in sense of "what can be said about," Late Han has yun-her 云何 . Both deeng and yun in these senses are innovations in Late Han.

Examples
Text 何人也 "what kind of person is he?" becomes 何等人也 (8.81); 不善之實何等也 "of what sort is the reality behind the word" 'bu-shan'?" (5.24). Text ru her 如何 "what can be said about it" becomes 其事云何 "of this happening, what can be said?" i.e. "what do you think about this matter?" (5.107). 鄉原之惡云何 "What can be said about the evil of the 'honest villagers'" (8.115) (Text has 何如). See also 2.50, 2.59, 2.61.

Note 1. Yun occurs in LAC to indicate quotation. In Late Han it occurs as a verb "to speak" as does wey 謂 in LAC, as, for example, 亦云大甚 "that, too, would be called excessive" (8.84); 孟子云 "Mencius said ..." (6.52, 7.27, etc.); hence yun-ho, 云何 "say what?" i.e. "what can be said about?"

Note 2. Her-you 何由 in LAC asks "from whence?" (see LAC 6.5.2.2). You 由 for "from" is obsolescent in Late Han (see section 3.5.ii above). Late Han uses you 由 in the sense of yong 用 and hence her-you 何由 in the sense of "of what use?" Examples are 教人治國不以其道則何由能治者乎 "If one were to instruct a man to govern the State contrary to the way [he has been taught], then of what use is his ability to govern?" (2.10); 侮奪之惡何由干之而錯其心 "The evils of arrogance and of acquisitiveness -- of what use is it to confound the mind by being involved in these things?" (4.110 (章)); 當以時修橋梁民何由病苦涉水乎 "He [i.e. Tzu-ch'an] should have repaired the bridges at the proper time and then what use would the people have for crossing rivers with such pain and suffering?" (5.6).

vi. Changes in the syntactical deployment
    of the Interrogative Substitutes

In LAC, pronominal substitutes occurring after the verb shift to the pre-verbal position when polarity is involved. In interrogative statements, the interrogative, in comparable deployment, also shifts to the pre-verbal position. In Late Han, this shift does not always occur.

Examples
Text 何謂 becomes 謂何 in 8.81, 2.70 (see also 2.79, 2.19, etc). See also preceding paragraph where her occurs after yun, viz. 云何.. Text 何以 becomes 以何 (6.52). Text 誰敬 "to whom should I show respect?" becomes 敬誰 (6.76). 誰先 "to whom should I give precedence?" becomes 先酌誰 "to whom should I give precedence when offering wine?" (6.77).

Note. This shift is consonant with the shifts occurring through the obsolescence of the negative/substitute/verb type of polarity (see section 3.6.i above).

vii. The use of Chii

Chii 豈 occurs in LAC where a question is rhetorical and anticipates a negative answer. Chii occurs in this usage also in Late Han, but the paraphrase often gratuitously adds chii where it is not in the Text. Chii, thus, is evidently current usage in Late Han.

Examples
Chii occurs in the Commentary but not in the Text in 7.57, 7.51, 6.52, 8.24, 8.73, 7.92, 8.30, etc. In 豈可得聞與 "May I hear about that?" (2.56), chii seems to be purely interrogative without the implication of an answer in the negative.

SUBSTITUTION

viii. The use of Tserng

Tserng 曾 occurs before bu 不 twice in the Commentary. Tserng is described in the Fang Yan (方言) as her-wey 何為 (see Tsyr-hae s.v. tserng). This appears to be the best interpretation to be placed on the following two examples: 剌邠君曾不如此鳥 "[The Duke of Chou, in writing this Song] wanted to needle [= criticize] the Prince of Pin [by asking] why did [he] not emulate this bird?" (2.87); 而曾不閔 "so why should he not mourn?" (7.15).

Note. The Tsyr-hae entry, quoted above, cites the Shin Fang-yan Shyh-tsyr 新方言釋詞 as authority for the suggestion that tzeen 怎 is a vulgar variant of tserng. Under tzeen, the Tsyr-hae notes that in T'ang poetry jeng 爭 is used for tzeen.

8.4.   SUBSTITUTION IN SUMMARY

| LAC | LATE HAN ||
	Changes in usage	Innovations in usage
焉；惡 and 惡呼 孰／誰 > 奚 > 何 何由 "from whence?" 何謂 etc. 豈	> 安 誰 > 何 何由 "of what use?" 謂何 etc. 豈 (in broader usage)	寧 "could?" >何等； 何人 etc. 曾 "why"

The interrogative substitutes, therefore, in common with other substitutes, share in the common shift away from specialized forms towards all-purpose forms, and in the tendency for the all-purpose forms to combine in compound forms.

CHAPTER 9

M I S C E L L A N E O U S

Other shifts and innovations in Late Han from LAC concern the degrees of comparison, the allegro forms, and enumeration. These are (i) new periphrastic means for indicating the degrees of comparison, and a tendency to mark comparison, where, in LAC, it is often unmarked; (ii) an avoidance of the use of allegro forms; (iii) the use of deeng 等 in the sense of "et cetera."

1. The Degrees of Comparison

The comparative and superlative degrees of comparison are as often as not unmarked in LAC, though LAC has the resources for marking them. In Late Han the degrees are more frequently marked, and new forms occur for marking them.

Preceding the attribute, LAC has jia 加 and yih 益. Late Han has also tzeng 增.

Examples
Text 民不加少 "My population does not get any larger" becomes 民人不增多於鄰國 "My population does not get any larger than my neighbours" (1.21); 益甚 "even more serious" (2.14) (see also 2.39); 而加撫恤之 "and sympathize the more with him" (1.78).

Following the attribute, with the particle of determination, LAC has jy shenn 之甚 ; jy jyh 之至 ; and jy you 之尤. Late Han avoids these formations and explains the use of jyh 至 in them as jyi 極 (5.103 and 4.80). Late Han prefers the inverted form.

Examples
至要 "most important" (2.58)
甚白 "very white" (3.112)
甚過 "very much in error" (7.52)

In the superlative degree, LAC has unmarked attributes. For example, <u>meei</u> = "lovely" in 牛山之木美矣 "The trees of Bull Mountain were once lovely" (6.102). <u>Meei</u> = "lovelier" or "better" in 膾炙與羊棗孰美 "Which is the better [eating], cooked meat or dates?" (8.105) and <u>meei</u> = "loveliest," "best" in 五穀者種之美者也 "The five grains are the best among plants" (6.129). <u>Meei</u> also occurs in an excessive degree "too lovely, too elegant" as in 木若以美然 "The wood, it seems, was too elegant" (3.1).

To mark the superlative degree Late Han has <u>tzuey</u> 最

Examples
<u>Text</u> 仁為美 "Humanity is its loveliest attribute" becomes 仁最其美者也 (2.102); <u>Text</u> 莫近焉 "Nothing is closer than that" becomes 最為近 "[This is] the closest" (7.75); 最為違禮 "running contrary to ritual, in an extreme degree" (8.83).

To mark the excessive degree, Late Han has <u>Tay</u> 泰太.

Examples
<u>Text</u> 木若以美然 "the wood, it seems, was too elegant" becomes 木若以泰美然也 (3.1); 齊宣王以三年之喪為太長久 "King Hsuan of Ch'i thought that three years of mourning was too long" (8.30). See also 太重 "too much" 太輕 "too little" (8.98); 太隘狹 "too narrow-minded" (2.112); 太過 "excessive" (2.82).

2. The Allegro Forms

In general the allegro forms of LAC, which combine in a portmanteau form two commonly associated particles, are either used in Late Han in blunted senses or become obsolete. The following is a list of allegro forms which occur in Text and Commentary:

LAC	LATE HAN
eel 爾 (而已)	prefers 耳 which is often used as a meaningless enclitic
eel 耳 (而已)	see above
fwu 夫 (否乎)	prefers foou hu
her 盍 (何不)	acceptable
her 曷 (? ?)	avoids
hwu 胡 (何故)	avoids
yan 焉 (於之)	avoids
in 因 (用以)	acceptable
ju 諸 (之於)	avoids
nae 乃 (若茲)	acceptable
ran 然 (如此)	avoids in non-combining sense, e.g. as "just so"
shi 奚 (何以)	avoids
u 惡 (何於)	avoids
yu 與 (也乎)	avoids
ye 邪 (也乎)	very common, but often, simply interrogative

3. Enumeration

In lists of names, where the list is not completed, Late Han uses deeng 等 "equal, on a par," as a sort of "et cetera," deeng substituting for the names unstated, but to be assumed by the reader. This is an innovation in Late Han.

4. MISCELLANEOUS IN SUMMARY

LAC	LATE HAN	
	Changes in usage	Innovations in usage
Jia 加 x; 益 yih x		tzeng 增 x 太, 泰, 最. deeng 等 "etc."

CHAPTER 10

CONCLUSION

Reviewing now the features described in chapters 2 - 9, the nature and extent of evolutionary change in the grammar of the language from the 3rd century B.C. to the 2nd century A.D. might be summarized as follows:

1. The "empty words" suffer loss in role and meaning. More specifically: (i) There is a diminution in the role played by "empty words" in making grammatical distinctions. (ii) There is a reduction in the number of distinctions made by the "empty words" and in the number itself of "empty words" employed and a tendency for those employed to be used in blunted or broadened senses. The trend is towards general all-purpose forms. (iii) There is semantic loss in certain "empty words" leading to their employment in parasitic or meaninglessly enclitic ways. (iv) There is also semantic shift in certain auxiliaries leading to shifts in role and deployment.

2. There is an increase in the use of periphrastic means to make grammatical distinctions. More specifically, the formal means of indicating the determinative role, of indicating mood, voice, and interrogation and the like, which are vested in the "empty words" of LAC, are replaced in Late Han by periphrasis, and new periphrastic forms occur.

3. The "full words" acquire enhanced significance. More specifically, the single word of LAC tends to be replaced by the compound word in Late Han and the compound word tends to greater restriction in grammatical deployment. Words customarily occur in _either_ nounal or verbal positions, and do not permutate.

A major evolutionary shift, therefore, occurs between the 3rd century B.C. and the 2nd century A.D. The "Archaic-Han Shift" is away from the precise, predictable, and meaningful use of the "empty words" and a reduction in their grammatical role, with a corresponding increase in the more precise indications and predictable deployment of the "full words". Quite clearly during these critical five hundred years a change of the greatest importance in the historical evolution of the language takes place. We might say that the traditional characterization of the grammatical auxiliaries of Chinese as "empty words" in Archaic Chinese is a misnomer, but that once the Archaic-Han Shift takes place, the characterization become appropriate. The seeming "modernity" of certain Han innovations has been remarked upon. What is here called the "Archaic-Han Shift" is towards features that are recognizably typical of Modern Standard Chinese.

But there is also a retrogressive tendency observable in the history of "Classical Chinese" in Han times. While writers like Jaw Chyi, and, later, the author of the Shyh-shuo Shin-yeu (世說新語) and the like, reflect, in their "easy wen-yan," the evolutionary movement in the language, others, like Ban Guh in Hann Shu and Jaw Chyi himself in the Chapter Summaries, in deference to canonical authority, embellish their writings with archaic forms and particles and follow an artificial metrical pattern in deliberate imitation of classical models. It is thanks therefore to the Commentary of Jaw Chyi that we can measure the extent of obsolescence, innovation, and change. If we had to depend upon the great Han Classicists, with their admixtures of the old and the new, the task would be much more difficult.

POSTSCRIPT

In paragraph iii of the Introduction to this book the statement is made that "a number of features have been described as 'Late Han innovations,' which must be understood in an accommodated sense. They are innovations in so far as Archaic Chinese is concerned, but they may well have antedated our Late Han author."

In the <u>Leu-shyh Chuen-chiou</u>, Mr. Ward informs me, a text which dates from the very close of the Late Archaic period, the following features occur, which elsewhere in this book have been described as Han innovations.

(i)   The introduction of the protasis in a conditional sequence, in the pre-agential position by 若 ; 使 ; 為 ; 若令 ; and 今使 . (cf. 7.2.i).

(ii) The use of 有閒 (cf. 5.5.ii).

(iii) The 被 and 為 passive (cf. 3.4.i).

(iv) The occurrence of "如...如..." for "either...or..." (cf. 4.2.i).

(v)   The use of 反 "on the contrary". (cf. 7.1.iii).

(vi) The use of 其卒 and 其餘. (cf. 2.3.iii).

(vii) The blunting of the 其 and 之 distinction. (cf. 2.2.i).

(viii) The use of 最 , and the occurrence of 甚 and 至 before attributes. (cf. 9.1).

With these exceptions, the <u>Leu-shyh Chuen-chiou</u> is, in every other linguistic respect, a typical Late Archaic document, as the transitions which its Late Han commentator Gau Yeou makes, testifies (see footnote 13).

APPENDIX 1

LATE HAN AND EARLY ARCHAIC CHINESE

The <u>Shu Jing</u> and the <u>Shy Jing</u>, which are Early Archaic texts, are frequently cited in <u>Mencius</u>, and, where such citations occur, Jaw Chyi in his <u>Commentary</u> translates them into Late Han.

His treatment of the grammatical auxiliaries of EAC is as follows:

Chapter and paragraph in Early Archaic Chinese	Early Archaic		Late Han	Reference in Mencius
	Shu Jing	Shy Jing		
Syntagma				
2.5		及	與	1.112
2.6.7.1	厥		其	1.90
2.6.7.3		靡	無	4.88
Verbal Sentence				
3.3.ii	丕		大	4.46
3.3.2.7	一		初	2.15
3.3.3.2		鄂	可	1.109
3.4	于	于	於	6.28, 4.30
			於	1.88
			從	6.28
3.4.5.1	越	自		2.85, 5.110
	自		皆	4.46
3.5.3	咸	聿	俱	1.113
		或	誰	2.87
3.5.3.1			無	6.28
	亡	莫	無有	5.100

Chapter and paragraph in Early Archaic Chinese	Early Archaic		Late Han	Reference in Mencius
	Shu Jing	Shy Jing		
3.5.4	胥	胥	相	1.98, 1.113, 4.96
3.5.5	β/del/ə'		del/β	1.89
3.6	其		以	1.89
3.7			而	3.56
3.9		其載普造于時	[辭也]	4.96
3.10			徧	5.100
			及	2.87
			於是時	1.86
Determinative Sentence				
4.2	惟		作	1.89
Inter-Sentential				
5.4.1	乃		由是	1.98
5.4.2	其		則	2.15
Substitution				
6.2	厥		其	1.90
		言	我	2.88
6.4	時		是大	1.18
6.5	害		何為	1.18
		爰為	何為	2.14
			何	1.88, 1.89
6.6	曷攸		何所	3.67, 4.28
Miscellaneous				
7		爰	於是	1.88, 1.113
			又以	1.110

APPENDIX I

In column four above, "Late Han," it will be seen that the language that Jaw Chyi uses for paraphrasing EAC is precisely the same language that he uses for paraphrasing LAC. Consistency and predictability are thus maintained throughout the Commentary.

A comparison of EAC and Late Han confirms the conclusions already drawn as to the nature of evolutionary change in the language from LAC to Late Han. The obsolescence of specialized forms of the pronouns and demonstratives, and the convergence upon all-purpose forms, are shown in the rendering of yan 言 jyue 厥 and shyr 時 by the all-purpose woo 我 chyi 其 and shyh 是 ; the distributives yuh 聿 and huoo 或 by the all-purpose, but blunted, jiu 俱 and shwei 誰 ; the interrogative and indefinite substitutes her 曷 shi-wey 奚 為 and iou 攸 by the all-purpose her 何 and suoo 所. The allegro forms are rendered in their discrete parts, for example, yuan 爰 by yu-shyh 於 是. The special negatives mii 靡 wang 亡 and moh 莫 are replaced by wu 無.

Jaw Chyi betrays a considerable understanding of both Early Archaic and of Late Archaic, but Archaic Chinese is not without its difficulties for him. He misunderstands the EAC hay 害 (allegro form of her-yii 何 以) rendering it as dah 大 "great." But he cites, in his Commentary, glosses on the Shy Jing of both the San Jia 三家 and the Mau 毛 schools (2.87, 1.113, etc.). He independently quotes from the Shu Jing (5.2, 5.30, 4.42, 3.95, etc.) and is familiar with the 古尚書 in 120 chapters (see 4.29 and 5.74). He cites the Tzuoo-juann (5.39, 2.131, 3.26, etc.); Analects (6.58, 3.46, 6.107, etc.); the Shiaw Jing (6.83); the Jou Lii (3.71, 3.73, 3.77, etc.), and the Yih Jing (7.53, 8.29, 8.78), in addition to his identifications of, and provision of references for,

citations from the Shu Jing and Shy Jing in the Text.[1]
We must suppose him to have been a well-read man.

---

[1] For the identification of the sources of Jaw Chyi's glosses I am indebted to the magnificent text-critical study of the text of Mencius and of the Jaw Chyi Commentary by Jiau Shyan (see footnote 13 above).

APPENDIX 2

THE NATURE OF LATE HAN CLASSICAL CHINESE

The language used by Jaw Chyi for paraphrase in his <u>Commentary</u> is quite different from the language he uses for the <u>Chapter Summaries</u> in which, at the close of each chapter, he points up the moral he wishes to draw from the <u>Text</u>. This difference in language I have characterized as Late Han Literary Chinese and Late Han Classical Chinese respectively.

Late Han Literary Chinese confines itself to contemporary grammatical forms, is free and uncontrived but prolix. Late Han Classical Chinese borrows from Archaic grammatical forms, is mannered, patterned, and terse.

Late Han Classical Chinese is restricted to a line of four stresses or of multiples of four - - eight or twelve - - with an introductory or concluding line which is metrically irregular. This metrical restriction imposes economy in the use of the "empty words." But when the "empty words" occur, they are drawn from a repertory composed, indifferently, of Early, Middle and Late Archaic forms, but also including contemporary forms. Late Han Classical Chinese therefore is not an attempt to imitate Archaic Chinese with any consistency, but a style in which Archaic features provide stylistic variants for contemporary features, thus providing a "classical" flavour.

In the <u>Chapter Summaries</u>, both Early and Late Archaic forms, which Jaw Chyi is so careful to avoid in the <u>Commentary</u>, are freely used. That they are used to achieve a "classical effect" is shown by their occasional occurrence in contexts where they are not, strictly speaking, appropriate. For example, the LAC tzyh 自 "from" which is avoided in the Commentary as obsolescent, and replaced by tsorng 從 "from," occurs in the Chapter Summaries as a variant for tsorng 從 "to follow," "conform with" etc., a usage which is foreign to LAC, but which derives from Jaw Chyi's definition of 自 as 從 (see 8.48 below). Examples of Archaic features used in Late Han Classical style are as follows:

1. Early Archaic Features

匪 ; in 匪禮之踰 for 非禮 "the excesses of improper Rites" (3.8 (章)) (see also 4.125).
攸 ; in 人倫攸敍 for 所敍 "the order in which human relationships are placed" (8.125 (章)).
茲 ; in 諸侯如茲 for 如此 "if the Feudal Lords behaved thus" (8.88 (章)).

2. Late Archaic Features

孰 ; in 孰敢不正 for 誰敢 "who dare not correct himself" (8.120 (章)).
自 ; in 不自王命 for 從命 "not according to the King's command" (8.48 (章)).
斯 ; in 亦斯類也 for 此類 "[these] too, are of this kind" (8.2 (章)).
諸 ; in 不反諸己 for 之於己 "not seek it in himself" (6.129 (章)).
弗 ; in 聖意弗珍 for 不珍 "the thoughts of the Sages were not prized" (1.70 (章)).
勿 ; in 惡而勿去 for 不去 "to hate it, yet not to leave" (4.83 (章)).

See also 斯亦 used for 此亦 ; (8.125 (章)).
自 used for 從 ; (4.83 (章)).
尚 used for 當 ; (8.38 (章)).
斯 used for 則 ; (7.77 (章)).

APPENDIX 2

3. Contemporary Features

但; in 非但免過 "it is not merely that he avoids error" (7.85 (章)).

凡; in 車絕乎凡 "far removed from the commonalty" (7.85 (章)).

應; in 應得其里 "must get the underlying reason for" (8.54 (章)).

須; in 仁恩須人 "for humanity and kindness there needs to be human beings" (8.66 (章)).

See also 俱 u.f. 皆 (6.121 (章)).

APPENDIX 3

LATE HAN AND MODERN STANDARD CHINESE

Karlgren, commenting on the occurrence of tzay 在 in the Luen Herng (論衡) as a post-verbal particle, notes that this is a feature of Modern Standard Chinese, and describes its appearance as early as Han as "a remarkable innovation."[1] A number of the innovations introduced in Late Han, following the Archaic-Han Shift, anticipate usages current in Modern Standard Chinese, of which the following are selected examples:

	LAC	Late Han	Modern Standard Chinese
不 弗 毋 勿 無	Mood and negation	不 [無 for 有] negation only	>	不 [没 for 有] negation only
		須 >	須要
		應 當 >	應當
且 當	potential >	且 暫 momentary momentary	> 暫且 "temporarily"
欲 "wish"		欲 "wish" 要 "wish" 欲 "will"	> 要 {"wish" / "will"}
既 已		> 已	> 已經

---

[1] See Bernard Karlgren, "Excursions in Chinese Grammar," BMFEA 23 (1951) p. 127, but on this, see also EAC 3.4.5.1, footnote 26.

APPENDIX 3

LAC	Late Han	Modern Standard Chinese
	但 "only" / "but"	但是 "but"
	即 "at once" 便 "at once"	立即 "at once" 便 "then"
見 (passive)	見 / 為 / 被 / (蒙)	見 / 被 / 蒙
於	於 / 在 >	在
自 "self" 自 "from"	> 自；自己 "self" > 從 "from"	自己 "self" 從 "from"
莫 (agential)	莫 negative	莫 negative (dial) cf. 没
或 (agential)	> 或...或... "either/or/" >	或是 "or"
孰 誰	} 誰	誰
相 (reciprocity)	相 > parasitic	parasitic in, e.g., 相信 "believe"
昨日 今日 明日	> 昨日 今日 明日 >	昨天 今天 明天
因 故	> 因：緣 故 緣 "deliberately" >	緣故 "reason" 故意的 "deliberately"

LAC	Late Han	Modern Standard Chinese
	就使 "if" >	就是 "then"
	儻 "suppose"	倘若（儻若） "even if"
最 太 }	before attribute	same
第	for ordinals	same

APPENDIX 4

JAW CHYI'S NOTIONS ABOUT LANGUAGE

Throughout the Commentary, Jaw Chyi gives lexicographical glosses on words in the Text and from these we can deduce something of his ideas about language.

Lexicographical glosses usually take the form of providing synonyms or near synonyms (for example 茲此也 "the word tzy 'this' is tsyy 'this'" (5.86) or 亡猶無也 "the word wang ('not present') is similar to wu (also 'not present' in certain contexts)") (6.129), or are descriptive, as, for example, 庠序者教化之宮也 "Shyang-shiuh are buildings used for teaching" (1.28), 數罟密網也密細之網所以捕小魚鼈者也 "Tsuh-guu are mih-woang, that is fine-meshed nets, nets with which small fish and turtles are caught" (1.24).

But words are also placed in classes, of which Jaw Chyi distinguishes, ming 名; cheng 稱; maw 貌; tsyr 辭; and sheng 聲 or in 音.

Ming 名 serves to denote personal names as in 盆成姓活名也 "P'en-ch'eng is the family name, K'uo the personal name" (8.88), but ming is also used for geographical names (for example 水名 "name of a river" (7.27); 地名 "place-name" (3.37)); and for the names of plants, for example 羊棗棗名也 "yang-tzao is the name of a date" (8.105). Ming is also used in 總名 for "generic name," as, for example, 械器之總名也 "Shieh is a general term for implements" (3.91).

Cheng is used for forms of address, particularly when such forms denote status, for example 公者國人尊君

之稱也 "<u>Gong</u> is a form of address used by subjects when showing deference to a prince" (3.39); 子男子之通稱也 "<u>Tzyy</u> is the common form of address to a male" (6.61); 叟長老之稱也猶父也 "<u>Soou</u> is a form of address to senior elderly people, rather like the use of <u>fuh</u> "father" " (1.5); 氓野人之稱 "<u>Min</u> is a way of referring to country folk" (3.83).

<u>Maw</u> is used for words which describe things metaphorically, as they appear to be or give the impression of being. <u>Maw</u> is used literally in 有若之貌 "Yu-jo's physical appearance" (3.112) but, in an extended sense, <u>maw</u> describes the function of the class of reduplicate (xx, xx-<u>ran</u>, and x-<u>ran</u>, see <u>LAC</u> 3.3.3.1) which describe manner metaphorically. For this usage Professor Demiéville has coined the word "impressif". For example, 濯濯然無草木之貌 "<u>Jwo-jwo</u> (lit. "as though scrubbed") describes the appearance presented by a lack of vegetation" (6.102); 蠡蠡欲絕之貌 "<u>Lii-lii</u> describes the impression given by something about to snap off" (8.72); 訑訑者自足其智不嗜善言之貌 "<u>yi-yi</u> describes the impression given by one who thinks his own wisdom all-sufficient and has no liking for good advice" (7.56); 晬然潤澤之貌 "<u>Tsuey-ran</u> means giving the appearance of having been anointed" (i.e., glowing, suffused, shining -- as in "it appears, with a glow, on the face") (7.99); 囂囂自得無欲之貌 "<u>Shiau-shiau</u> means giving an impression of contentment, of having no desires" (7.81); 圉圉魚在水羸芳之貌 "<u>Yeu-yeu</u> (lit. "a corral" and thus "corralled") describes the appearance of a fish entangled in the water" (5.88); 赧赧然面赤心不征貌也 "<u>naan-naan-ran</u> means red in the face, it describes the appearance presented when all is not right in the heart" (4.38); 望望然慚愧之貌也 "<u>wanq-wanq-ran</u> describes the manner affected by one who feels mortified" (2.107).

APPENDIX 4

Sheng 聲 and in 音 describe onomatopoeia, as, for example, 填鼓音也 "tyan is the sound made by a drum" (1.22); 閧鬭聲也 "honq is the hubbub of battle" (2.19). In 2.53 施 in the name 孟施舍 is glossed as 發音也 "a prefix marking phonetic attack."

Tsyr denotes a word in a very general sense. The following are defined simply as tsyr: fwu 夫 (8.22); eel 爾 (5.85); wei 惟 (4.15); guh 固 (1.64); yueh 曰 (1.5); chyh 翅 (7.4). Tann-tsyr 歎辭 "sigh-word" denotes an interjection, as in 夫歎辭也 "Fwu is an interjection" (6.64) and as in 於音烏歎辭也 "於 is pronounced like 烏, it is an interjection" (7.3); and as in 惡者不安事之歎辭 "U is an interjection expressing unease" (2.74) (in 2.121 u is described as a deep sigh); 爾歎而不怨之辭 "Eel is an interjection but has no suggestion of resentment" (8.123).

Tsyr is also used when a word is described by the function it performs. For example 云爾絕語之辭也 "yun-eel are words that mark a break in speech" (2.121). 焉耳者懇至之辭 "The words yan eel are used to indicate emphatic finality" (1.20). Words with overtones of status are called 謙辭, as for example 亦聖人之謙辭 explaining the occurrence of chieh 竊 in the Text, "a word indicating self-deprecation on the Sage's part" (5.35), and in explaining 竊聞 in the Text: 故謙辭言竊聞也 "And so, using self-deprecating words, he says 'chieh wen'" (3.75). Another way of referring to status words is 君臣上下之辭 "words differentiating prince and subject, superior and inferior," as in 1.10, where 國 "state" and 家 "estate" are said to belong to this class of words.

Jaw Chyi thus distinguishes between "words" tsyr and "non-words" sheng and in (i.e. onomatopoeic or non-phon-

emic sounds), and among "words" segregates names <u>ming</u>
- - both personal, proper, and generic names - -; social
appelations <u>cheng</u> which have to do with the social usage
of language; and words which describe manner <u>maw</u>.

Words are definable by replacement (with synonyms or
near synonyms), by description, or by function.

In linguistic terms Jaw Chyi is aware of the part
played by status in language, distinguishes between
phonemic and non-phonemic sounds, but apart from the
recognition of a class of proper names, of status forms,
and of a special form of attribute, regards the entire
lexicon as a single undifferentiated whole.

LIST OF WORKS MENTIONED

Chmielewski, Janusz
    "Notes on Early Chinese Logic (II)."
        Rocznik Orientalistyczny XXVl: 2 (1963) 91-105.

Dobson, W.A.C.H.
    Late Archaic Chinese: A Grammatical Study
        (Toronto, 1959).
    Early Archaic Chinese: A Descriptive Grammar
        (Toronto, 1962).
    "Studies in the Grammar of Early Archaic Chinese.
        I, The Particle WEI." T'oung Pao, 46 (1958)
        339-368.
    "Studies in the Grammar of Early Archaic Chinese.
        II, The Word JO." T'oung Pao, 47 (1959)
        281-293.
    "Towards a Historical Treatment of the Grammar of
        Archaic Chinese. I, Early Archaic Yüeh 越 >
        Late Archaic Chi 及." Harvard Journal of
        Asiatic Studies, 23 (1960) 5-18.
    "Studies in Middle Archaic Chinese. The Spring and
        Autumn Annals." T'oung Pao, 50 (1963) 221-238.
    "Word Classes or Distributional Classes in Archaic
        Chinese"; in L'Hommage à Monsieur Demiéville
        (in press)

Jiau Shyun 焦循
    Meng-tzyy Jenq-yih (孟子正義); in 國學基本叢書簡篇 Commercial Press (Shanghai, n.d.).

Karlgren, B.
    "Excursions in Chinese Grammar." Bulletin of the
        Museum of Far Eastern Antiquities, Stockholm,
        23 (1951) 107-133.

Karlgren, B.
　　Grammata Serica Recensa (Stockholm 1957).

Leu Shwu-shiang (呂叔湘)
　　Hann-yeu yeu-faa Luenn-wen Jyi (漢語語法論文集)
　　　　(Peking, 1955).

Yang Shuh-dar (楊樹達)
　　Tsyr Chyuan (詞詮) (Shanghai, 1928).

Yoshikawa Kōjirō (translated by Glen W. Baxter)
　　"The Shih-shuo Hsin-yü and Six Dynasties Prose
　　　　Style." Harvard Journal of Asiatic Studies, 18
　　　　(1955), 124-141.

Wang Shean (王顯)
　　"Shy-jing jong gen chorng-yan tzuoh-yonq shiang-
　　　　dang-de Yeou-tzyh shyh, Chyi-tzyh shyh, Sy-tzyh
　　　　shyh, her Sy-tzyh shyh 詩經中跟重言作用相當的有字式, 其字式, 斯字式, 合思字式
　　　　Yeu-yan Yan-jiou 語言研究 4 (1959), 9-43.

INDEX OF WORDS
treated at some length

AN	安	Replacing 焉, 惡, 惡呼 and in Late Han	8.3.i
BEEN-YOU	本由	As replacement for 始	5.5.ii
BEY	被	As periphrastic passive	3.4.ii
		Deployment of	3.4.ii Note
BIANN	便	Aspectual Determinant "at once"	3.2.vi
BIANN	徧	See Appendix I	
BIH	必	In 必不, intensive negative	3.1.iii
		In 必須, "must have or be"	3.1.viii
		Before verbs: "decidedly, inevitably, of a certainty." Negated by 不 and 未 In 當必. Injunctive before verbs	3.1.viii Note
BU	不	As all-purpose negative in Late Han	3.1.i
		In 不須.	3.1.viii
		In "不/verb/pronoun or demonstrative"	3.6.i
		As Sentential Modal particle. (See also 5.4.i)	5.4.iii
		In 不復 as conjunction	7.1.i

CHARNG	常	As replacement for 固	3.1.v
CHERNG	誠	As Conditional Conjunction. Replaces 苟 and 信. As modal determinant replaces 信.	7.2.ii
CHIEE	且	In Momentary Aspect "for time being," "at that time." In Potential Aspect "about to." In 方且: 暫且.	3.2.i
		As Conjunction.	7.1
CHII	豈	As replacement for 莫	4.2.i
		As replacement for 惡	8.3.i
		As Interrogative in Late Han.	8.3.vii
CHIING	頃	In Time phrases.	5.5.ii
CHU	初	See Appendix I	
CHYI	其	Confused with 之	2.2.i
		As demonstrative "this, this sort of"	2.3.ii
		In 其實 and 其終	2.3.iii
		Before certain nouns = "other"	2.3.iv
		Relationship with 斯	2.3.iv Note
		As Agentive Pronoun	4.1.i
		Reduced role in anaphora. (See also 8.1.ii; Appendix I.)	5.3.i

INDEX OF WORDS

DANG	當	As marker of the Injunctive Mood	3.1.vii
		As verb "assume responsibility for, take office as, be equal to, or adequate for"	3.1.vii Note ii
		In 當必	3.1.viii
		As Conditional Conjunction	7.2.iv
DANN	但	Before nouns, "only"	2.4.ii
		Before verbs, restrictive aspect"	3.2.iv
		As polar form of 不	3.2.v
		<u>Dann</u> and the adversative (see also 7.1.i)	3.2.v Note
		<u>Dann</u> and polarity	3.6.ii
		As copula, also in 非但; and 但為 (see also Appendix II)	6.1.i
DAY	迨	See Appendix I	
DEEI	得	As marker of the Injunctive Mood	3.1.iv
DEENG	等	In 何等	8.3.v
		As "et cetera"	9.2
DWU	獨	In 獨身	4.5.i
EEL	耳	As sentential modal particle in Late Han	5.4.i

EEL	爾	In 爾之 as determinative pronoun in Late Han	2.1.i
		Obsolete as agentive pronoun in Late Han	4.1.i
		As allegro form obsolete in Late Han (see also 8.1.i)	5.4.i
ERL	而	Reduction of role in Late Han	5.1.i
		Parasitic occurrence in Instrumental phrase	5.2.i
		As adversative and simple connective conjunction (see also Appendix I)	7.1.ii
ERL-YII-YIH 而已矣		Replacement by 也 or 耳	5.4.i
FAAN	反	As conjunction "on the contrary" (see also footnote 1, 7.1.iii)	7.1.iii
FANG	方	In Momentary Aspect, also in 方且	3.2.i
FARN	凡	In Late Han > "commonplace, ordinary" (see Appendix II)	2.4.i
FEEI	匪	See Appendix II	
FOOU	否	Obsolescent in Late Han in pregnant usage	5.4.ii
		As Interrogative Sentential modal particle (see also 5.4.i)	5.4.iii

INDEX OF WORDS

FU	夫	Obsolete as allegro form in Late Han	5.4
FUH	復	In Iterative Aspect, in Durative Aspect, as verb = "revive, restore" in 新復 "newly," before numerals "a further," and in parasitic usage	3.2.ii
		As Conjunction	7.1.i
FWU	弗	Replacement by 不	3.1.i
		In "弗/verb/demonstrative" (see Appendix II)	3.6.i
GONG	躬	As Agential Distributive, also occurs in 躬身	4.5.i
GOA-REN	寡人	Obsolescent in Late Han	8.1.i Note
GOOU	苟	Obsolescent in Late Han as Conditional Conjunction	7.2.ii
GU	姑	Replacement by 且	3.2.i
GUEY	貴	Replacement for modal 有	3.1.vi
GUH	固	Obsolescence in modal role in Late Han and replacement by 常 and 素	3.1.v
		Confusion with 故 and 古	3.1.v Note
GUH	故	Confusion with 固 and 古	3.1.v Note
GUOO	果	Obsolescence in modal role in Late Han and replacement by 能 and 竟	3.1.v
		Use in 果穀	
		Glossed as 克	3.1.v Note

GUU	古	Confusion with 固, 故	3.1.v
HAY	害	See Appendix I	
HER	何	Assimilates 奚, 曷 and 胡	8.3.iv
		Expanded as 何等, 何人, 云何 etc.	
		Substitutes for 焉	8.3.i
		In 何由 "of what use?" (see also Appendix I)	8.3.v Note
HER	曷	Obsolescence in Late Han (see also Appendix I)	8.3
HU	乎	Obsolescence in Late Han as post-verbal particle	3.4.v
		Loss of precision in Late Han as final particle	5.4.i
HUOH	或	Obsolescence as Agential Distributive in Late Han. Occurrence in 或 ... 或 ... formations (see also Appendix I)	4.2.i
HWU	胡	Obsolescence in Late Han	8.3
I	一	See Appendix I	
IN	因	Introducing causal clauses	6.2
ING	應	See Appendix II	
IOU	攸	See Appendixes I and II	
JANN	暫	Momentary aspect, also occurs in 暫且	3.2.i
JEA	假	In 假使 as Conditional Conjunction	7.2.i

INDEX OF WORDS

JEE	者	As marker of causal clauses	2.5.i
JER	輒	As Aspect "on each occasion" also occurs in 每輒	3.2.vii
JIA	加	In the degrees of comparison	9.1
JIANN	見	In periphrastic passive	3.4.i
		Deployment of	3.4.ii Note
JIAU	交	Obsolescence in Late Han as marker of reciprocity: Assimilation by 俱	4.3.i
JIE	皆	As Agential Distributive, post-verbal collective, and encroachment 皆 by 俱 (see also Appendix I)	4.2.ii
JIE	偕	Obsolescence in Late Han and replacement by 俱	4.2.ii
JIH	既	Replacement by 已	3.2.ii
		As marker of subordinate clause in Late Han	5.1.ii
JII	己	As Agent in 己自	4.5.i
		As Emphatic and Reflexive Pronoun, also occurs in 己身, 己自, 自己	4.5.ii
		As replacement for 之	8.1.ii
JINQ	竟	As replacement for 杲	3.1.v
		In Time phrases "finally"	5.5.ii

127

JINQ-BU	竟不	As intensive negative	3.1.iii
JIOW	就	As Conditional Conjunction and as verb "come or go"	7.2.v
JIOW	舊	Used for 故	3.1.v Note
JIU	俱	As Agential Distributive encroaches upon 皆	4.2.ii
		As post-verbal collective	4.2.iii
		Encroachment upon 交 as marker of Reciprocity (see also Appendixes I and II)	4.3.i Note
JU	諸	In blunted usage as anaphoric pronoun in Late Han	5.3.ii
		Obsolescence as allegro form in Late Han (see also Appendix II)	5.4.i
JY	之	Occurrence between pronoun and noun	2.1.i
		Confusion with 其	2.2.i
		Occurrence between attribute and noun	2.6.i
		Reduced role in anaphora (see also 4.1.i and 8.1.i)	5.3.i
JYH	至	In Degrees of Comparison	9.1
JYI	即	In aspect "at once"	3.2.vi
		As copula	6.1.iii
JYI	及	See Appendix I	

INDEX OF WORDS

129

JYUE	厥	See Appendix I	
KEE	可	Modal function of (see also Appendix I)	3.1.ix
KEE	鄂	See Appendix I	
KEH	克	Gloss for 果	3.1.v Note
LINQ	令	In periphrastic causative and permissive	3.4.iv
MEEI	每	In 每輒	3.2.vii
MENG	蒙	In periphrastic passive	3.4.ii
MII	靡	See Appendix I	
MOH	莫	As negative in blunted usage	3.1.ii
		Obsolescence as Agential Distributive (see also Appendix I)	4.2.i
NAE	乃	See Appendix I	
NENG	能	As replacement for 果	3.1.v
		Modal function of	3.1.ix
NINQ	寧	As verb "bring peace to," as Interrogative substitute "could, can?"	8.3.ii
PI	丕	See Appendix I	
PIH	譬	Occurrence in 譬如; 譬若; 譬猶 etc.	6.1.iv
PUU	普	See Appendix I	
RAN	然	Obsolescence in pregnant usage	5.4.ii

RU	如	As replacement for 由	3.5.ii Note
		As replacement for 而	5.1.i
		In 譬如	6.1.iv
		As Conditional Conjunction, also occurs in 如使	7.2.i
RUOH	若	As replacement for 由	3.5.ii Note
		As selective conjunction	4.2.i Note
		In 譬若	6.1.iv
RUU	汝	Determinative form of	2.1.i
		As Agential pronoun (see also 8.1.i)	4.1.i
SHANQ	尚	Injunctive in 尚當 etc.	3.1.vii
		Replaces 猶 as concessive conjunction	7.3.iii
		Following a noun = "even a" (see also Appendix II)	
SHEN	身	An Agential Distributive, also occurs in 自身; 身自 and 獨身	4.5.i
SHENN	甚	In the Degrees of Comparison	9.1
SHI	奚	Obsolescent in Late Han and replacement by 何, and 何為	8.3.iv
SHIANG	相	Marker of reciprocity, also in parasitic usage (see also Appendix I)	4.3.i

INDEX OF WORDS

SHINN	信	Obsolescence as Conditional Conjunction in Late Han and replacement by 誠	7.2.ii
SHIU	須	As marker of Injunctive Mood, as verb "should have or be", and occurrence in 不須; and 必須 (see also Appendix II)	3.1.viii
SHIU	胥	See Appendix I	
SHIU-YU	須臾	In Time phrases	5.5.ii
SHU-WU	殊無	As Intensive Negative	3.1.iii
SHWEI	誰	Assimilates 孰 (see also Appendix I)	8.3.iii
SHWU	孰	Obsolescence in Late Han and assimilation into 誰 (see also 8.3.iii and Appendix II)	4.2.iv
SHYAN	咸	As Agential Collective in Late Han (see also Appendix I)	4.2.v
SHYH-YIH	是亦	As replacement for 而	5.1.i
SHYH	是	As demonstrative, in determinant usage with 之 (see also 6.1.i Note)	2.3.i
		As copula	6.1.i
SHYI	昔	Obsolescence in Late Han	5.5.i
SHYR	時	See Appendix I	

SHYY 使	In periphrastic causative and permissive	3.4.iv
	As Conditional Conjunction, also occurs in 如使; and 假使	7.2.i
SHYY 始	Defined as 本由	5.5.ii
SUH 素	As replacement for 固, used for "habitually, formerly"	3.1.iv
SUOO 所	See Appendix I	
SY 斯	Obsolescence as Determinative Demonstrative in Late Han	2.3.i
	Relationship with 其 "<u>Attribute/Sy</u>" interpreted as reduplication	2.3.iv Note 3.3.ii
	Obsolescence as Conditional Conjunction in Late Han (see also 8.2 and Appendix II)	7.2.iii
TA 他	Before nouns "other" 他日 replaced by 異日	2.3.iv 5.5.ii
TAANG 儻	As Concessive Conjunction, for required condition	7.3.ii
TING 聽	As verb "to let or allow"	3.4.iv
TSERNG 曾	As Interrogative Substitute in Late Han	8.3.viii

INDEX OF WORDS

TSORNG	從	Replacement for 自	3.5.i
		Replacement for 由 (see also Appendix I)	3.5.ii
TSYY	此	In Determinant usage with 之	2.3.i
		As Conditional Conjunction	7.2.iv
		In 此物; 此人 and 此事 replacing 之	8.1.ii
TZAI	哉	See 5.4.i	
TZAI	載	See Appendix I	
TZAY	在	As post-verbal particle, also in 在於	3.4.v
		Use in EAC	3.4.v Note
TZENG	增	In the Degrees of Comparison	9.1
TZER	則	As replacement for 而	5.1.i
		In 則復 as conjunction	7.1.i
		As replacement for 斯 as Conditional Conjunction (see also Appendix I)	7.2.iii
TZUEY	最	As marker of superlative degree	9.1
TZWO	昨	In 昨日 "yesterday"	5.5.i
TZWU	卒	In Time phrases	5.5.ii
TZY	茲	See Appendix II	
TZYH	自	Replaced by 從	3.5.i
		As Agential Distributive, also occurring in 躬自; 自身; 身自; 己身; 自己	4.5.i

TZYH	In word-formation, as "self"	4.5.i
	As Concessive Conjunction in Late Han (see also Appendixes I and II)	7.3.i
U, U-HU 惡: 惡呼	As Interrogative Substitute obsolescent in Late Han and replaced by 安 or 何	8.3.i
WANG 亡	See Appendix I	
WEI 惟	See Appendix I	
WEI 爲	Obsolescence of modal role	3.1.vi
	In periphrastic passive constructions	3.4.iii
	Deployment in periphrastic passive	3.4.iii Note
WEY 謂	Used for 爲 in 以爲, 所以...爲 and for 爲 as a verb	4.4.i
WEY 未	Replacement by 不	3.1.i
	Replacement by 無 before 有	3.1.i Note
	Blunted usage of	3.1.ii
	Before verbs and numerals "not yet"	3.1.iv
	In "未/verb/pronoun" constructions	3.6.i
WEY JIAN 爲間	Obsolescence in Late Han	5.5.ii

INDEX OF WORDS

WOANG	往	Replaces 昔 in Late Han and used in 往者 and 往日.	5.5.i
WOO	我	In 我之 as determinative pronoun in Late Han	2.1.i
		As Agential form (see also 8.1.i) (see also Appendix I)	4.1.i
WU	吾	In 吾之 as determinative pronoun in Late Han	2.1.i
		Obsolescence as Agential pronoun (see also 8.1.i)	4.1.i
WU	無	Replacement by 不	3.1.i
		Negation for 有	3.1.i Note
		In "Wu/verb/pronoun" constructions	3.6.i
		As replacement for 莫 (see also Appendix I)	
WU	毋	See 3.1.i	
WUH	勿	Replacement by 不	3.1.i
		In blunted usage	3.1.ii
		In wuh/verb/pronoun constructions (see Appendix II)	3.6.i
YAN	焉	Blunting of usage as anaphoric pronoun in Late Han	5.3.ii
		As Interrogative replaced by 安	8.3.i

YAN	言	See Appendix I	
YE	邪	As general marker of the Interrogative in Late Han	5.4.i
YEE	也	In blunted usage	5.4.i
YEOU	有	Negation by 無	3.1.i Note
		Obsolescence as modal and replacement by 貴	3.1.iv
		Before an attribute, interpreted as reduplication of attribute	3.3.ii
		Replacement for 或 (see also Appendix I)	4.2.i
YEU	與	See Appendix I	
YI	宜	As injunctive before verbs	3.1.viii
YI-CHIEE	一切	As "momentarily"	3.2.i Note
YIH	已	For perfective aspect	3.2.ii
YIH	益	In the degrees of comparison	9.1
YIH	亦	As conjunction	7.1.i
YIH-RYH	異日	As replacement for 他日	5.5.ii
YII	矣	In blunted usage	5.4.i
YII	以	As replacement for 而 in Late Han (see also Appendix I)	5.1.i

INDEX OF WORDS

YOU	由	Replacement by 從	3.5.ii
		Replacement by 如 and 若	3.5.ii Note
		Occurrence in 譬由 (see also 6.1.iv)	3.5.ii Note
		Obsolescence of modal role	3.5.ii Note
		Use as verb "to use, follow" and occurrence in 何由 for "of what use?" (see also Appendix I)	3.5.ii Note
YOU	猶	Replaced by 復 for durative aspect	3.2.iii
		Obsolescent as Concessive Conjunction in Late Han and replacement by 尚	7.3.iii
YOW	又	Replacement by 復 for Iterative Aspect in Late Han	3.2.iii
		As conjunction occasionally replaced by 復 in Late Han	7.1.i
YU	于	Obsolescent in Late Han as post-verbal particle (see also Appendix I)	3.4.v
YU	與	Obsolescent as allegro form in Late Han	5.4.i
YU	於	As marker of the Locative	3.4
		Occurrence in 在於 (see also Appendix I)	3.4.v

YUAN	緣	Introducing causal clauses	6.2.i
		Before verbs "deliberately, of set purpose"	6.2.i
YUAN	爰	See Appendix I	
YUEH	越	See Appendix I	
YUH	欲	In Potential Aspect "about to" and in Desiderative Aspect "wish to"	3.2.i
		Occurrence in 且欲 and 將欲	3.2.i
YUH	聿	See Appendix I	
YUN	云	In 云何 and as verb "to say"	8.3.v